A Guide to Counselling and Basic Psychotherapy

To   E., C. & M.

'....whatever fortune brings,
Don't be afraid of doing things.'
(Especially, of course, for Kings.)

A Guide to Counselling and Basic Psychotherapy

By

RICHARD PARRY

M.B., M.R.C.P., M.R.C. Psych., D.P.M.
Consultant Psychiatrist, Royal Edinburgh Hospital.
Senior Lecturer, Department of Psychiatry, University
of Edinburgh.

CHURCHILL LIVINGSTONE
EDINBURGH LONDON AND NEW YORK
1975

CHURCHILL LIVINGSTONE
Medical Division of Longman Group Limited

Distributed in the United States of America by
Longman Inc., New York, and by associated companies, branches and representatives throughout
the world.

© LONGMAN GROUP LIMITED 1975

ISBN 0 443 01281 4

Printed in Hong Kong

Preface

My undergraduate interest in psychiatry evaporated during my clinical years, as it does for many medical students, when I encountered psychiatrists and psychiatric patients. It was re-awakened during six years of general practice during which I had the opportunity of attending one of the seminars for general practitioners organised by the late Dr Michael Balint and his colleagues at the Tavistock Clinic.

This had the unexpected but not absolutely unique consequence of leading me to suppose that I was a better psychiatrist than the psychiatrists, and I decided to specialise. Perhaps psychiatry's loss has been general practice's gain. In consequence I have fallen into many of the pitfalls of psychotherapy and have sometimes seen others fall in after me. I decided, therefore to introduce some order into my own practice, partly in the hope that others as well as myself might learn something from my mistakes.

This book is, therefore, really an account of some of the guidelines used by one man in his psychotherapeutic work. They are certainly not the only guidelines, neither are they necessarily the best ones. It is not easy always to adhere to them, and it may be a comfort to the reader, as it is to the author, to know that in their time, some of the greatest therapists, have strayed from the ideal.

It is hoped that the book may be of value to the medical student, particularly during his clinical years. It would best be studied during his course on psychiatry, as a supplement to his standard text book, for at this stage he may be interested in acquiring some psycho-therapeutic skills. Perhaps too it will be of value to other doctors, especially to general practitioners, to psychiatrists at the beginning of their training, and to members of other professions which run parallel to medicine and especially psychiatry: nurses, social workers, occupa-tional therapists and clinical psychologists.

I have another important group in mind. This comprises the in-creasing number of people who offer some sort of counselling, either as part of their own profession (clergymen, welfare officers, etc.) or in a voluntary capacity (Marriage Guidance Counsellors, Samaritans, etc.). These people often use skills which are similar to those employed by the psychotherapist, just as physiotherapists and osteopaths may use techniques which were developed by specialists in physical medicine.

It may be surprising to learn that the book has no clearly stated theoretical basis. I have in fact used only those concepts which are acceptable to most theoretical schools. I assume the existence of unconscious mechanisms, that there is a part of the personality which is called the conscience, and that some people may have incestuous thoughts and feelings.

Only very limited use has been made of case histories, and these are fictional or apocryphal. I have not used the experience of specific patients known to me, but because patients may have rather similar experiences, some may think that they recognise themselves or others. The only non-fictional character is the author himself, and he has been considerably romanticised.

It must be conceded that psychotherapy is not in the high regard of many psychiatrists at the present time—indeed, many take a great deal of trouble to demonstrate that, not only is it of no value, but that in some cases, it may actually be harmful. These criticisms must be taken very seriously, but unfortunately, it is not always clear what is meant by the word 'psychotherapy'. Until the subject can be defined more precisely, the criticisms can neither be confirmed nor corrected. I hope that this book may add one small straw to the wind of definition.

Many people have helped me in the preparation of this work—albeit unknowingly. They include my friends, my foes, my family; my professors, my pupils, my patients and my publishers. They are really so numerous that it would be invidious to pick out a few in particular. They all have my sincere thanks.

Edinburgh, 1975   R.A.P.

Acknowledgements

The author wishes to express his gratitude to the following authors and publishers, for permission to quote from copyright material:

Ernest Benn Ltd., for an extract from *Psychopathology Of Everyday Life* by Sigmund Freud, Ed. James Strachey.

Michael Flanders Esq., for 'The Spider': words by Michael Flanders. Recorded in 'The Bestiary Of Flanders and Swann'. Parlophone PCS 3026.

W.H. Freeman and Co. and the Editor of *Scientific American*, for the dialogue from 'Doctor-Patient Communication' by Barbara M. Korsch and Vida Francis Negrete.

Hutchinson and Co. Ltd., for an extract from *The Prince who Hiccupped* by Anthony Armstrong.

The Editor of the *Lancet*, for the definition of *Le Bovarysme* by Forfar and Benhaman.

Methuen's Children's Books and Mr. C.R. Milne, for 'Happiness', from *When We Were Very Young* by A.A. Milne.

Frederick Muller Ltd., for an extract from *Maybe You're Just Inferior* by Herald Froy.

Sigmund Freud Copyrights Ltd., for the letter from Freud quoted in *Life and Work of Sigmund Freud* by Ernest Jones.

The Society of Authors on behalf of the Bernard Shaw Estate, for two extracts from *Pygmalion* by Bernard Shaw.

Contents

Contents

Introduction

'Psychotherapy is, above all, not theoretical knowledge, but a personal skill.' Michael Balint 'The doctor, his patient and the illness'.

The high ambition of this book is to teach the student nothing that he does not already know. This became the author's intention when, at the end of the course on which it is based, a member of the class said 'You have not told me anything new, but you have made me think about it'.

'Thinking about it' is the first stage of the 'limited but considerable change in the doctor's personality' which Balint considered to be an essential in the acquisition of psychotherapeutic skill. The development of the skill requires practise, and whilst a book can offer some guidelines and indicate the pitfalls it cannot replace actual experience. In his 'Introductory lectures on psycho-analysis' Freud reminded his audience that by listening to him they would not learn 'how to set about a psycho-analytic investigation or how to carry the treatment through'. Operative surgery provides a suitable parallel. No book can teach the surgeon how to proceed in an individual case, but it may supplement his own experience and the examples of his teachers.

The medical student's first contact with patients occurs when he learns to take a case history. It is then that he begins to observe the patient—and to be aware of the patient's observation of him. The art of careful history taking is without doubt a matter of prime importance. There are few diseases in which a careful history does not reveal the diagnosis. It is confirmed subsequently by physical examination. Symptoms are seldom preceded by physical signs. As a result of history taking, the student will for example, learn to differentiate between organic heart disease and a neurotic preoccupation with cardiac function. It is a matter of regret that history taking frequently ceases at this point. Many investigations might be avoided and much anxiety alleviated if, as the result of a few more questions, the reasons for the neurotic preoccupation could be elicited.

The influence of a doctor upon his patient is tolerated in these days of scientific medicine as an inevitable but regrettable distraction. Ingenious methods are devised in an attempt to eliminate it from therapeutic trials—or at least to neutralise it. Doctors often feel slightly dishonest when they use their relationship with him for the benefit of the patient and prefer to ascribe the credit to a placebo reaction. But the influence of the 'bedside manner' cannot be denied.

Balint formulated the useful proposition that the doctor himself could be thought of as a potent drug which may be used for good or ill. He emphasised the care with which the doctor must be 'dispensed'. The aim of this book is partly to help the reader define the nature of this 'drug' and to use it in a way which will be helpful to himself and beneficial to his patients. There is no wish to define it for him.

So far we have spoken about the relationship between a doctor and his patient, but others also relate to patients. Furthermore, not everyone who needs the assistance of a helpful relationship is a patient. Nurses, social workers, occupational therapists, clinical psychologists, and other members of the para-medical professions may exert a powerful influence on their patients and they must learn to employ this influence to its maximum effect. Other people too, sometimes counsel: they may be church workers, welfare officers or members of one of the voluntary organisations such as the Marriage Guidance Council or the Samaritans. It is hoped that the methods described here may be of value to them also.

Lest it should be questioned that a book designed primarily for doctors should be offered also to non-medical workers, it may be pleaded that treatment is not the exclusive prerogative of doctors. The same general methods may be used by workers in other fields as well as the medical one. For example, simple therapy for colds, coughs and constipation may be suggested by pharmacists and herbalists as well as by doctors. It is, however, hoped that if the non-medical or voluntary worker finds that he has undertaken something which appears to be beyond his capacity, he will seek the help of a professional adviser.

1.   No Man is an Island...*

CARDINAL PRINCIPLE—There is nothing so obvious that it can be accepted without question.

The cardinal principle is an axiom of medicine. Its corollary is that there is nothing so absurd that it may be dismissed without consideration, and together they form a cardinal principle for psychotherapy and counselling. The intention of this book is to counsel about psychotherapy. The cardinal principle must therefore be applied. Nothing that is written, however obvious, may be accepted without question. The reader should dispute all that he reads. He may even dispute the cardinal principle.

There are multitudes of people who seek help and advice from others in this world. Sometimes their difficulties are concrete and may be specified precisely: more often they are the vague and indefinable problems of everyday living. Coincidental with the demand for advice, various organisations have developed which offer assistance, counselling or treatment in personal difficulties. They and their clients often turn for help to doctors and to members of the para-medical professions —to whom the gift of omniscience is traditionally ascribed. Guidance may be sought on problems of which the practitioner knows little or nothing; but the doctor who pleads ignorance will be regarded as being merely modest. Advice will be read into whatever he says, so he must be careful of the way in which he says it. Even when he is knowledgeable, it is not necessarily easy for him to phrase his advice in a way which will be helpful to the patient. Here is the transcript of an interview in which a paediatrician fails to help two very worried parents†:

FATHER :   How does his heart sound?

DOCTOR :   Sounds pretty good. He's got a little murmur there. I'm not sure what it is. It's...it er...could just be a little hole in his heart.

MOTHER :   Is that very dangerous, when you have a hole in your heart?

---

*...entire of itself; every man is a piece of the Continent, a part of the main.' John Donne, Devotions XVII.

†from 'Doctor-Patient Communication', Korsch and Negrete, *Scientific American*, August 1972. **227:2** p.68.

DOCTOR: No, because I think it's the upper chamber, and if it's the upper chamber then it means nothing.

MOTHER: Oh.

DOCTOR: Otherwise they just grow up and they repair them.

MOTHER: What would cause the hole in his heart?

DOCTOR: H'm?

MOTHER: What was it that caused the hole in his heart?

DOCTOR: It's cause...er...just developmental, when their er...

MOTHER: M-h'm.

DOCTOR: There's a little membrane that comes down, and if it's the upper chamber there's a membrane that comes down, one from each direction. And sometimes they don't quite meet, and so there's either a hole at the top or a hole at the bottom and then...it's really...er...almost never causes any trouble.

MOTHER: Oh.

DOCTOR: It's er...one thing that they never get S.B.E. from...it's the only heart lesion in which they don't.

MOTHER: Uh-huh.

DOCTOR: And er...they grow up to be normal.

MOTHER: Oh, good.

DOCTOR: And er...if anything happens, they can always catheterize them and make sure that's what it is, or do heart surgery.

MOTHER: Yes...

DOCTOR: Really no problem with it. They almost never get into trouble, so...

MOTHER: Do you think he might have developed the murmur being that my husband and I both have a murmur?

DOCTOR: No.

MOTHER: No? Oh, it's not hereditary, then?

DOCTOR: No.

MOTHER: Oh, I see.

DOCTOR: It is true, that certain people...tendency to rheumatic fever, for instance.

MOTHER: M'mm?

DOCTOR: There is a tendency for the abnormal antigen-antibody reactions to be inherited, and therefore they can sometimes be more susceptible.

MOTHER: Oh, I see. That wouldn't mean anything if er...I would...

I'm Rh negative and he's positive. It wouldn't mean anything in that line, would it?

DOCTOR: No.

MOTHER: No? Good.

DOCTOR: No. The only thing you have to worry about is other babies.

MOTHER: M-h'm?

DOCTOR: Watch your Coombs and things.

MOTHER: Watch my what?

DOCTOR: Your titres...Coombs titres.

MOTHER: Oh, yes.

The reader may wish to read this transcript again, and to consider what makes it so unhelpful.

Now we shall turn to a group of people who have problems of various sorts, and consider briefly whether anything can be done to help them.

Mrs Burton

Mrs Burton is a married woman in her early thirties. She has long straight hair, very dark, with streaks of grey. Her figure is trim and she dresses well. Her skin is slightly greasy. She has made an appointment with a counselling agency and has arrived thirty minutes early. The previous client has cancelled his appointment and in consequence the counsellor is able to see her immediately. She is rather taken aback at being ushered straight into the consulting room and says with a touch of anxiety 'I am not late am I? My appointment was for...'. The counsellor explains what has happened and shows her to a chair. When both are seated he asks 'Tell me what the trouble is'.

Mrs Burton replies in an attractive, soft, well-modulated voice. She tells her story very concisely, as though it has been rehearsed carefully. Briefly, it boils down to this. Her husband, who is an executive, a little older than herself, is drinking heavily. She fears that he may be turning into an alcoholic. She says that she can stand it no longer, and unless he does something she will leave him. He does nothing. What should she do?

Well, what should she do? Should she find an outside interest, or get a job, or make herself more attractive? Should she flirt with other men, to make him jealous? Should she ask her doctor for a tranquilliser? Should she start drinking with him? Should she make sure that he is never alone? Should she ask a relative to give him a good talking-to? Should she remember that at least her husband is working, and that there are many people in the world who are far worse off than she? Should she buy some provocative underwear? Should she be reassured that in the end, everything will probably come right?

At this point the reader should pause to consider these and other possible alternatives.

The information Mrs Burton has given is very precise, and if she means what she has said, there is only one course open to her. Very gently the counsellor points this out. 'It sounds as though you must leave him, Mrs Burton,' he says. She bursts into tears, 'I can't possibly do that, I love him. Besides, there are the children. Can't you do something?' She goes on to tell of two friends who have attended the agency and of how much they have been helped.

The counsellor is touched by her tears, and wants to help her very much. After all, he joined the agency in order to help people. 'Perhaps you can tell me a little more' he says. Mrs Burton continues with her well-rehearsed story.

Let us consider this case for a moment. Mrs Burton has a problem. It arises out of the relationship between two people, her husband and herself. Problems always arise between people. They never arise between people and things. 'People' may be one, two, or many. They may be intimates or ill-defined groups. They may be parents, children, spouses, friends. They may be the Coloureds, the Jews, the Russians or the Government. They are people whose needs or behaviour differ from those of the patient.

When problems exist between people and things, a solution can be achieved swiftly and painlessly. An inanimate object may be removed, a dress discarded, a house exchanged. But if the thing has a human association, the other parties have to be considered. The dress may have been bought by a loved partner. It may not be the house which is wrong, but the people who live in it. The *solution* of a problem also involves people. Mrs Burton hopes that the solution to her problem will emerge through the person of her counsellor. She will assume that he knows of many cases such as her own. If he fails to offer a simple solution, she may feel that for some reason or another he is being deliberately unhelpful.

It should be noticed that the problem also involves feelings. When a problem arises between people, feelings are induced in them. When there are no feelings there is no problem: there never was, because they would have drifted apart.

All sorts of feelings may be inferred from Mrs Burton's case. Most obvious is her love for her husband and her sadness that for some reason her love is not reciprocated—for if it were, surely he would stop drinking. There is anger with her husband, which she may wish to deny, saying 'I am not angry with him, it is the alcohol . . .'. There is the sense of helplessness for herself and for her children—that is why she has sought advice. She will surely have feelings about the counsellor, who has offered her the one piece of advice she did not want.

Another point may be considered also. The counsellor has no solution to offer which had not been examined previously and rejected by the client herself. The counsellor has no secret untried paths along which he can guide his client. All the alternatives are either painful or useless, and they have been rejected. Sherlock Holmes once said that 'When you have eliminated the impossible, whatever remains, *however improbable*, must be the truth', and to paraphrase him, when everything that is impracticable has been eliminated, whatever remains, however unpalatable, must be the solution. The counsellor cannot *tell* Mrs Burton what to do. He can do nothing more than consider the alternatives with her. He has no quick solution, no anaesthesia, no medicine that will solve her difficulty.

Before Mrs Burton has completed her story, the counsellor's next client is waiting, and he says that it will be necessary to stop. He is rather relieved by this, because he is not quite sure what to do, and feels that he himself is in need of help. He assures Mrs Burton that the story can be continued at their next meeting, and she is given another appointment.

The counsellor has been impressed by Mrs Burton. Her personality is an attractive one, and he is very anxious to help her. But he can see no glimmer of hope in the story which she has given. He wonders if this might be the sort of case which is handled better by someone with more experience. He decides to discuss the problem with the agency's psychiatric adviser.

The counsellor and the psychiatric adviser are friends, and when the counsellor telephones him in the evening, the psychiatrist notes some familiarities in the story. On consulting his files he finds that he had himself seen the client some months previously. Mr Burton had been referred by his family doctor because of his drinking habits. The doctor had asked for 'help with this distressing case'. Mr Burton had ignored the offer of an appointment, and Mrs Burton had come instead. When he had heard the story, the psychiatrist said that he could do nothing unless Mr Burton attended in person. Otherwise he saw no alternative to separation. He did not offer another appointment and Mrs Burton was too frightened to ask for one. She feared that some pressure might be brought upon her to leave her husband and this was the last thing she wanted.

The psychiatrist remembered Mrs Burton very well. He too had found her personality an attractive one. He was touched by her story. He wanted to help his friend the counsellor. And he thought that the case might be a useful illustration for a book he was writing.

Dr Kildare is an assistant in general practice. He finds that his patients expect him to know everything about medicine, and about all sorts of other things as well. They bring the most complex problems to him, but he seldom knows what to do or what to say. The advice he gives often appears to be trite and superficial, yet they come back.

A patient will come into his consulting room, complaining of a symptom. Whilst he is thinking of the possible causes, she (it is more often a she) suggests an explanation. She says 'Do you think it could be because...'. Then she embarks upon a very long and extremely complicated story involving her family, her friends, her neighbours, and her household. Dr Kildare listens attentively, but to tell the truth, he can make neither head nor tail of her story. Totally bewildered, he terminates the consultation in a way hallowed by medical tradition. He gives the patient a prescription for a tonic, and tells her to return in a week's time.

This she does. She begins by thanking him for all the advice which he offered her at their previous meeting. She says she has done exactly what he suggested, that in consequence all her symptoms have disappeared, and she has not required the tonic. She returns the prescription to him. Dr Kildare is very puzzled. He cannot remember having given any advice. He can remember only being rather confused and baffled by the whole thing, and his slight feeling of irritation at having to listen to something which seemed quite unrelated to the task for which he had been trained.

One day he comes upon a book which claims to guide him about counselling and psychotherapy. He hopes that this will throw some light on the problem.

A young doctor is commencing his career as a psychiatrist. When his friends ask him if he goes around psychoanalysing everyone he meets, he coughs modestly. He has spent a considerable amount of time with his next patient and is anxious to impress his superiors with his success in treating her. At the sixth session she bursts into tears. She does not have a handkerchief, and his is rather crumpled. Between her sobs she says 'According to Dr Parry's book you should always have a box of paper handkerchiefs available'. The young doctor blushes.

A middle-aged woman has joined a voluntary counselling agency. She says that her own marriage has been a very happy one, and she would like to help people less fortunate than herself. In fact her own marriage has not been particularly successful, and seems to be getting worse rather than better. Much to her relief, the people who have selected her do not seem to know this. She feared that they might have some secret way of finding out. Many of her clients are in a position similar to her own, and neither she nor her colleagues seem to do very much to help them. Desperately, she turns to a book on counselling and psychotherapy. It is of no help, either, and she throws it aside in disgust, 'It seems just to be trying to turn people into amateur psychiatrists' she says.

A consultant surgeon storms into his operating theatre 20 minutes late. He is in a terrible temper, and comes upon a student nurse reading a book on counselling and psychotherapy. He snatches it from her and hurls it across the ante-room. 'Show me the evidence' he roars, 'show me the evidence!' The nurse bursts into tears.

A patient comes for his umpteenth appointment with his psychiatrist. 'I read your book' he says. 'I thought it was by someone else. It has nothing whatsoever to do with what goes on here. It's typically arrogant of you to tell people what they ought to do. Why don't you practise what you preach!'

No therapy can succeed unless therapist and patient can look at a problem from the same viewpoint. The patient will usually describe a situation exactly as he sees it. He will describe it 'truthfully'. However, on objective examination of the whole, there may prove to be other truths or even contradictory ones. What seems 'true' to the patient may seem 'false' to those around him. The therapist must be able to perceive the truth not only from the point of view of the patient, but also from that of those whose relationship with the patient has led to the problem. Let us examine these six small cameos and try to understand a little more of what is going on.

We will begin with Dr Kildare, who feels so inadequate for the role which seems to be expected of him. In the first place, his patients attribute to him a far greater knowledge of medicine than he possesses, and expect him to be much more worldly-wise than he knows he is. Despite this, they seem to get better. He feels the need of a much older head on his shoulders. He thinks that others would quickly know how and what to do. He hopes to find the wisdom he needs in a book. He will be disappointed, for whilst it may supplement it, there is no book in the world which will replace his own experience.

The young psychiatrist knows this sense of inadequacy too. Success is very important to him. He feels that his superiors will judge him by it, although their criteria of success are not necessarily the same as his.

He is not prepared for an unforeseen situation when the patient bursts into tears, and when she reproaches him for not conducting his sessions according to Dr Parry's book, the young psychiatrist is embarrassed. He is anxious lest his hard work should come to nothing, and is more than a little irritated with Dr Parry for having written a book which a patient can quote at him. However, he must not forget that this is the sixth session which his patient has attended, and this behaviour alone indicates a desire for help. Her attendance indicates respect and affection for the person who is trying to help her. The doctor has said that she may say anything she likes. She will observe how he responds to her remonstrance very carefully. Did he really mean she could say *anything* she wishes?

The voluntary counsellor is in need of help. She had hoped to solve her marital problem in a roundabout way, avoiding the very people to whom she should turn. She is ashamed to admit her failure, and has ignored the fact that a physician really must heal himself before he can help others. She has been dishonest with her selectors, and is dishonest even with herself. When she fails to find the answer she seeks either in her work or in a book, she rejects both, convincing herself that the fault lies in them.

The consultant surgeon is a very lonely man, shy of people and uncertain of himself. He roars because he fears scornful rejection if he is too gentle. He likes to think of himself as an objective scientist, because he does not understand the intimacies of personal relationships, and is rather frightened by them. No-one will ask him why he was 20 minutes late, and he will never volunteer the reason. It is because his only friend has had a heart attack, and he has spent some time at the bedside.

Dr Parry's patient is angry with him and hostile. Perhaps things are going badly, and he seeks a scapegoat, so he challenges him to practise what he preaches. Dr Parry is a little hurt by this, because he has tried very hard. However, he knows that the patient has attended his sessions regularly, and that his antipathy is not sufficient to turn him away, although he may disparage what occurs as insincere, unreliable and unhelpful. There seem to be other more positive emotions, and Dr Parry must be as careful as he can be, not to show that he is offended.

Now let us return to Mrs Burton. Her problem is a complicated one and involves several other people. It appears to be insoluble. She loves her husband and does not want to leave him, but she cannot stand his drinking, and in consequence feels that she cannot remain with him. She had asked the psychiatrist for a solution to this impasse, but he gave her none. She feels that there must be someone, somewhere, who can show her the answer. She thinks of two friends who received help in equally unpromising situations.

The counsellor's problem arises from Mrs Burton's. He likes his client and would like to help her. He enjoys his work and wishes to be proficient at it. He wants to feel successful in what he has undertaken and has been put on his mettle: two of his colleagues have been praised for the help which they were able to give to their clients, and he would like to equal their achievements. Perhaps there is a hint of rivalry in his ambition to do well, and if he is wise he will consider this possibility very carefully. But at present he can see no solution to Mrs Burton's problem. On one hand, there is the irresistible force of the wife's wish to remain with her husband—provided he does not drink—and, on the other, is the immovable determination of the husband to continue his way of life. Surely, thinks the counsellor, there must be some way out of this dilemma. Surely there must be someone who can show it to him.

Mrs Burton's family doctor also had a problem. His patient came for help, but for one reason or another he was unable to provide what was required. Perhaps he felt a trifle irritated by this exposure of his limitations. He tries to conceal his irritation from Mrs Burton and particularly from the psychiatrist, by the use of a phrase which offers a rather facile combination of compassion with irony, 'I should be glad of your help in this distressing case'.

The psychiatrist has a problem. The counsellor has demonstrated his belief that the adviser may have some secret way out of the difficulty. They are friends and the psychiatrist is anxious to help him. He remembers Mrs Burton and would like to help her too, but he knows there are no secret paths, no-one in the world, no-one who has ever lived who can solve the problem as it stands. Perhaps a little too tender-hearted to say this to Mrs Burton directly, he indicates that he can do nothing unless the patient, the 'sick' person who was actually referred to him, attends. To tell the truth he doubts whether anything can be done, even if he does attend. Unless Mr Burton himself wishes to do something about the problem which exists between his wife and himself, nothing will happen.

There are other matters to be considered. Mrs Burton has an unrealistic and totally unjustified belief that somehow, from the depths of his experience, the counsellor will find a solution to an insoluble problem. The counsellor has the same expectation of the psychiatrist. Mrs Burton's family doctor supposes it would be worth a try, although he would really be very surprised if anything did come from the consultation. There is a strong suggestion that the psychiatrist's interest in the case is more in its value as a piece of illustrative material than as a terrible hurt, arising out of the crumbling relationship between two people. Problem always arise between people. Happiness or sadness is a result of the interaction between one person and another. Fear, anxiety, terror, pleasure: emotions always arise out of the relationship between people.

Terminology

The words, patient, therapist, counsellor, client, psychotherapy and counselling have been used, and it is necessary to differentiate between them. The distinction lies in the relationship between the parties involved.

When the relationship is a *treatment* one, the words patient and therapist may be used. The procedure is called psychotherapy, although the therapist may sometimes think that this is a rather grandiose word for a simple consultation. The therapist is a doctor or a member of a medical team, such as a nurse, a social worker, a clinical psychologist, or an occupational therapist. The patient may present with a personal problem. At other times, because he fears that personal problems may not be the proper concern of medical practice, he may present with a symptom: usually with a psychological one, such as insomnia or depression, occasionally with a physical one, such as headache or dyspepsia.

When the relationship is a *counselling* one, the terms counsellor and client should be used. The counsellor is not a therapist and should not claim to be one. In cases where treatment may be needed, the counsellor will seek the advice of a medical practitioner. The counsellor may be, for example, a minister of religion, a lawyer, a welfare officer, or a member of one of the voluntary organisations such as the Marriage Guidance Council or the Samaritans.

The terms client and counsellor are not altogether satisfactory ones. The word 'counsellor' may conjure up the image of a bearded sage, an ancient of infinite wisdom—a sort of Solomon—or perhaps an American lawyer. The word client is used indiscriminately for anyone who uses the services of a bank, a bookmaker or a prostitute. Unfortunately, satisfactory alternatives do not appear to exist.

Confusion arises because the psychotherapist and the counsellor use roughly the same approach, and the 'sickness' of the patient may be identical with the 'problem' of a client. The counsellor may think of himself (not necessarily with justification), as an inferior therapist and the therapist as a sort of superior counsellor.

Types of Counselling and Psychotherapy

There are two basic types: intensive and supportive. In this book, intensive psychotherapy will be dealt with principally. The aim of intensive psychotherapy is to help the patient change his way of life, to examine those aspects of his behaviour which are irrational, inappropriate or irrelevant and to help him develop more realistic forms. Intensive psychotherapy and intensive counselling are creative attempts to assist the patient recognise the maladaptive aspects of his personality so that he can, if he wishes, take appropriate steps to modify them. Intensive counselling and intensive psychotherapy involves work which is arduous, difficult, uncomfortable and often fascinating. For the patient it involves an intense self-scrutiny which may be disconcerting, disagreeable, and even painful. For some people the cure is worse than the disease, and not everyone is willing or able to submit himself to such intense examination.

There is another form of counselling and psychotherapy which is called 'supportive' and which will be mentioned briefly. Supportive counselling and supportive psychotherapy is provided for those people who are unsuitable for intensive therapy. Perhaps they are of unstable or inadequate personality or have no particular intelligence. They often seem content with their neurotic way of life and show no serious desire to change it. They derive some gratification from spending a short while with their counsellor or therapist, but no-one really expects them to change, and no great efforts are made to help them do so. The patient attends briefly, perhaps once a month or sometimes only once in three months. During his session he describes the difficulties which he has encountered whilst the therapist tries to listen attentively—although to tell the truth his mind may wander on to more agreeable topics. At the end of the session the therapist draws together a few threads, reassures his patient and dismisses him until his next visit. It is hoped that the patient will derive some benefit from being 'supported'. No real effort is made to change the status quo.

Everyone involved in counselling and psychotherapy carries a certain number of people such as these, knowing well that they are really doing very little for them. They would often be very willing to pass them on to someone else, but since most therapists have a similar burden, it is never easy to find other shoulders. Sometimes the patients seem to derive benefit from their brief sessions, and there are often some details of technique to be learned from them. Working with them is part of the price that must be paid for the more gratifying intensive work. In this book, supportive psychotherapy will not be considered to any extent.

Schools of Psychotherapy

The principles described here do not follow those of any particular 'school' of psychotherapy. They 'borrow' whatever may be useful from all. When psychotherapy or counselling is based on a broad but indeterminate basis it is usually described as 'eclectic'. The specific 'schools' of psychotherapy are built upon a firm theoretical structure and three will be described briefly.

The best known is that which emanates from the work of Sigmund Freud, and the technique is known as Psycho-analysis. It supposes that the mature personality emerges out of the progression of certain basic drives through three stages of development. In the early years of life these drives are focussed in turn on the mouth, the excretory apparatus and the genitalia. Psychological abnormality and psychiatric illness is thought to be due to either a failure to mature beyond a certain point, or to regression to an earlier one. The total theory forms, by virtue of its completeness and its logical development, an attractive and coherent whole. Some people think that it puts too much strain on the maxim that there is nothing so absurd that it can be rejected without consideration. Psycho-analysis is the most intensive type of psychotherapy available. The patient meets his therapist every day for about an hour, and treatment may continue for several years. The couch is used. Particular attention is paid to the vicissitudes of the sexual instinct, and especially to the way in which it manifests itself early in life. The aim of therapy is to achieve a total reconstruction of the personality. Psycho-analytical treatment can be provided only by analysts who themselves have undergone a formidable period of training. Owing to the scarcity of such practitioners, their concentration in certain geographical areas, the length of treatment, and its very high cost (it is not available under the N.H.S.) only a very few patients can benefit from it.

Psycho-analysis examines the adaptation of the individual to his environment. A culture is seen as the product of those of whom it is comprised. Complementary to this point of view have developed, particularly in the United States, a group of 'Neo-Freudian' schools in which there is a shift of emphasis. They pay more attention to modification of the individual by the environment. Individuals are a product of the culture in which they live. The Neo-Freudian schools have emerged from classical psycho-analysis, but their theoretical basis is less precise.

Alfred Adler was at first an associate of Freud, but in due course he rejected much of Freud's teaching and founded his own school, which bears the name, 'Individual Psychology'. Adler and his co-workers paid particular attention to the *total* and habitual 'way of life' of the patient. This is given the name of the 'life-style'. The life-style originates from an individual's endeavours to compensate for areas of weakness of which he has been aware from his earliest years. Adlerians pay close attention to their patient's total life pattern, and endeavour to identify similar patterns of behaviour in differing situations. In this respect, Individual Psychology has importance for psychotherapists of all schools. The aim of therapy is to change the life-style—a goal which is probably more convincing in theory than in practice. It has an essential simplicity which appeals to those who have a naive view of humanity.

The school of Analytical Psychology was founded by Carl Jung, another associate of Freud and the only member of the trio who had the decency to be a Christian. Jung was a wise and sensitive man of great knowledge and wide experience, and his principles have found particular acceptance from those whose framework is a religious one. Much of Jungian psychotherapy is concerned with analysis of what is called the 'collective unconscious': the deepest part of the unconscious which is supposed to be inherited by one generation from the previous one. The theory involves much that is mystic, speculative and unverifiable, and the author has not found Jungian concepts of great help in his own work. Others seem to find them useful.

2. Patient and Therapist

CARDINAL PRINCIPLE: People are people.

Selection of Patient

Sherlock Holmes had many of the attributes of the ideal psycho-therapist and in this book we will meet him more than once. Watson described him as 'the most perfect reasoning and observing machine that the world has ever seen'. Although he had astonishing gaps in his education (he did not know that the earth moves round the sun), he knew everything about his own subject. When he was confronted with a new problem he was usually able to refer to others like it. He would say, 'you will find parallel cases in Andover in '77 and there was something of the sort at The Hague last year'.

But Holmes is one of the immortals and was created omniscient. Therapists and their patients are people, and being only people their powers are limited. Sam Weller had a similar point to make, although in a slightly different context. In the course of his cross-examination during the trial of Bardell v. Pickwick he was asked by Counsel for Mrs Bardell, 'You were in the passage, and yet saw nothing of what was going forward. Have you a pair of eyes, Mr Weller?' With the most complete simplicity and equanimity of manner, Sam replied 'Yes, I have a pair of eyes, and that's just it. If they wos a pair o' patent double million magnifyin' gas microscopes of hextra power, p'raps I might be able to see through a flight o' stairs and a deal door; but bein' only eyes, you see, my wision's limited'.

Although we think of them by different names, the therapist and his patient are only people, and psychotherapy is, at its simplest, people trying to help people. The similarities between the patient and his therapist are much greater than their differences: they are psychologically similar just as they are physically similar. They are likely to have similar hopes and fears, desires, prejudices and weaknesses. They usually come from the same culture. The things of which they are ashamed will probably be similar, they will be ambitious for similar goals; and will share similar illogicalities.

Many people have a high (but unwarranted) expectation of psycho-therapy, seeing it as a panacea for all ills to which flesh is heir, a cure for everything which cannot be coped with by other forms of treatment. Such hopes are, of course, absurd. A few practitioners see it as a convenient dumping ground for troublesome patients, and a handy scapegoat when they are not thereby made trouble-free. Psychotherapy makes very few claims for itself. It certainly does not aspire to make the bad good, the idle industrious, or to change cowards into heroes. It will not make dullards brainy, short people tall, or turn brunettes into blondes. It does not aim to make silk purses from sows' ears. The therapist will endeavour to help the patient make the most of such assets as he has. He offers no guarantee of success, and if the patient is helped his therapist will not suppose that there will be no remaining problems when therapy is terminated. He will hope for only limited improvement in exchange for much hard work.

Problems are commonplace but psychotherapists are few. It is therefore proper that they should select their patients with care, and work principally with those who have the best prognosis. This is an inevitable practice if a particular skill is at a premium. No surgeon would offer a renal transplant to a man in his 70's, neither would anyone expect a person who is mentally handicapped to embark upon a university course. No matter how much people such as these would like to profit from an opportunity which is offered to others, they must seek alternative help. It is hard on those who are rejected for intensive psychotherapy and may seem unfair. But questions of 'fairness' or 'unfairness' should not normally influence medical decisions, which must be based on objective realities. The truth may appear to be unfair, but the fact is that the truth is the truth.

Motivation

When the therapist considers the problem of motivation, he endeavours to answer the question 'What does this patient really seek when he asks for psychotherapy?' It has been stressed already that no promises can be given as to the outcome of psychotherapy, and that treatment is complicated and prolonged. Facts such as these must be understood and assimilated by the patient before he can even be considered a possible candidate. It would be easy for him to attend periodically, outside his working hours, provided that there were no other distractions; provided that he was not feeling too tired, and provided that an ambulance was supplied to take him to and fro. Easy enough—in fact far too easy. The patient who is a candidate for psychotherapy will certainly have to submit himself to considerable inconvenience. Within reason, he will be expected to attend during the *therapist's* working hours, not during his own free ones. If he has a more attractive engagement, he must forego it in favour of therapy. Therapy is sometimes unpleasant, sometimes disquieting, anxiety provoking, demoralising, sometimes depressing. It may be boring, apparently aimless, fruitless, perhaps infuriating. There will be occasions when the therapist will appear obstinate, unsympathetic, objectionable, offensive, impertinent, hostile, sadistic, unnecessarily pedantic. At times, psychotherapy can be one of the most painful procedures under the sun, and what is more, there is no analgesic with which the pain may be alleviated.

These obstacles have not been exaggerated in any way. The difficulties of psychotherapy are formidable. It follows that it will be offered only to patients who are very strongly motivated indeed. Their motivation will be subjected to intensive scrutiny, and sometimes put to the test.

The mere assurance that 'I will do anything to get better' is not of itself sufficient. Patients may say anything, especially if subjected to external pressures, to alleviate their discomfort. A man whose wife has left him will promise anything if he hopes that by doing so he will persuade her to return. The employee who has been warned a dozen times will, when he is finally discharged, protest that he has at last realised the error of his ways and that if he is given just one more chance, he will promise to take the necessary steps to reform. The prisoner who has made a sexual assault on a child will suddenly realise that he is in urgent need of treatment, and will promise to do anything— even to 'go into a mental institution' if, by doing so, he will avoid punishment.

When motivation springs from external pressures such as these, it will be regarded with considerable suspicion. No matter how passionate may be the pleas in such circumstances it is usually best to allow the dreaded event to occur, and to offer treatment afterwards. It is vital that psychotherapy should not be regarded as a soft alternative to punishment. The child molester who truly realises that he needs treatment will not lose that realisation as the result of a period of imprisonment, and if he wishes, he may be considered for treatment when he has completed his sentence. Unhappily his motivation is then frequently exposed for the pretence it truly was. Motivation which arises from external pressures is suspect and the therapist need have no hesitation in discussing this fact with a potential patient. The patient whose motivation is sincere will understand that it must be so, and will be willing to return after the disaster has passed. The patient who responds with offended indignation that he should be 'suspected', and who sees the discussion as an attack on his probity, will naturally cause serious doubts to enter the mind of the therapist.

When external pressures appear to be trivial or absent, the therapist must endeavour to assess the strength of the internal ones. Certainly these may be sufficient to urge the patient to accept the difficulties of psychotherapy, despite its own inherent discomforts.

The assessment of internal pressures depends partly on an appraisal of the history: partly on an intuitive appraisal by the therapist. What has the patient done on his own account to solve his difficulties? If his efforts have been confined to asking his doctor for sleeping tablets and tranquillisers, a certificate to the local authority asking for alternative housing and one for his employers requesting a change of job, he is merely demonstrating his intention to leave the work to others, so that he himself can continue a life of cosy convenience. Conversely, the patient who has shown himself prepared to undertake a difficult task and to follow it through, or who has endeavoured to do so, certainly displays a sense of independent purpose. The patient who acknowledges that he is himself partly responsible for his misfortunes shows a readiness, at least to regard himself as fallible, compared with the grandiose infallibility of the man who always blames others. People who wish to maintain a view of themselves as innocent victims of someone else's failings are not good subjects for psychotherapy.

Sometimes it is appropriate for the therapist to set a small task as a test of motivation. The heavy drinker may be asked to abstain from alcohol totally (i.e. totally) for a given period—perhaps one month—and then to return to report on his success. Some patients will truly make an effort. They may not be successful, but that does not matter too much. Others will not even try. They may say 'Why should I? I like it. Anyway, I am not an alcoholic'. Patients whose response to such a test is 'Why should I', show themselves to be unwilling to suffer any discomfort or inconvenience. They are unlikely to be satisfactory candidates for intensive psychotherapy. It may be suggested to an alcoholic whose motivation is suspect, that he attend meetings of Alcoholics Anonymous regularly for a period. Again the patient who declines, perhaps saying 'I don't like them' is unlikely to persist with psychotherapy, which will inevitably involve a great deal of what he does not like.

Sometimes a deficiency of motivation becomes apparent only after psychotherapy has commenced. The patient arrives late repeatedly, or offers a trivial or sometimes apparently genuine excuse for failing to attend. ('I forgot': 'I had to work late': 'It was my birthday': 'There was an earthquake': etc.) When this happens the patient's motivation may be discussed with him. If it is inadequate he may take advantage of the discussion to terminate treatment and at the same time make it appear that the responsibility is that of the therapist. ('Well if you think I don't want to come, I won't. . . .'). The therapist may have spent many sessions with his patient before the lack of motivation becomes apparent, but nevertheless, in circumstances such as these, he would be best to terminate. Time will not necessarily have been wasted, because the seeds of insight may have been planted in the preliminary sessions, and motivation will grow from them. If psychotherapy is terminated in this way it may be possible for it to be resumed if circumstances change.

Sometimes, it becomes apparent that a patient has been attending because someone else has told him to do so. He will feel that he is, in some way, being forced to do something that he does not wish. He may not be quite sure whether or not he is attending of his own free will. When this happens, he may behave in a way which indicates that he now wishes to withdraw. He should usually be allowed to do so. If he sees that his attendance is under his own control, that there is no *force majeure,* that he comes of his own free will, he may be very willing to resume.

We have spoken of motivation as though it were something that is either present or absent, but in fact it seldom occurs in such a black and white fashion. There may be positive motivating forces such as the 'pain' of the problem and the desire for relief, but negative ones may operate too. ('If things don't work out I will blame the therapist.') There may be motivating forces which are only indirectly relevant to the problem, such as curiosity about what psychotherapy is like. There may be the self-indulgent pleasure of having an uncritical, captive, audience.

Ultimately the therapist must endeavour to identify, as precisely as possible, the motivating forces, the counteracting ones, the balance between them and their ultimate direction. In some of this he will be forced to rely on his intuition which can, of course, be exceedingly fallible. He will in part be affected by his attitude towards the patient (see counter-transference, page 64). Some of his assessments will be incorrect but others will be triumphantly accurate. Time and experience will be needed for him to improve his accuracy. He need not be unduly dispirited if at first he is wrong, rather more frequently than he would wish.

Intelligence

In the course of therapy it will be necessary for the patient to consider his past experiences; to examine his recurrent patterns of behaviour; to ponder the possible symbolism of some of his experiences, and to think about the various ways in which he reacts to his therapist. For this, at least a moderate degree of intelligence is required. Psycho-therapy is not likely to be very rewarding with the dull, even though their I.Q. may be within the limits of normal. A prospective patient for intensive psychotherapy should have been able (provided that he had had the opportunity of doing so) to pass at least one or two 'O' level subjects. Paradoxically, high intelligence is not a particular advantage in psychotherapy, and patients should not be selected for this reason alone. Indeed, a high I.Q. may sometimes be an obstacle to successful living. The problems of some people of high intelligence may arise directly from their ability to perceive conclusions far ahead of their fellows. And just as I.Q. cannot be increased in those who are dull, neither can it be lowered in those who are bright. It is not always easy to realise that people of high intelligence are not necessarily good therapeutic prospects, but the fact remains. In the absence of adequate motivation, they may take a perverse and sometimes destructive delight in running rings round their therapist. This point must be emphasised because many people feel that very intelligent individuals *should* be able to get to grips with their problems. Experience repeatedly demonstrates that this is not necessarily the case, and such a conclusion must always be carefully questioned.

Age

Many people start their career as psychotherapists or counsellors with a wish to work with young people. This is very understandable. The young are often lively, attractive and enquiring, and it is a great pleasure to watch them mature. However, many of their problems arise from immaturity and are automatically resolved as they grow older. The therapist who accompanies them through this process may be pleased to take the credit for the improvement which occurs. He thereby enjoys the credit of success, when it is really due to nature.

In cases where problems are experienced by young people, more help may be required by the parents than by the young person himself and it is preferable that, at least at the beginning of his training, the therapist should practise his craft on older people rather than younger. It is a matter of considerable experience to distinguish between those young people who are likely to improve as a result of maturation, and those who need expert help. Such experience cannot be gained until some time has been served as a 'bread and butter' therapist.

It is often stated that the 'old' are unsuitable for intensive therapy. Someone who has been set in his way of life for many years will not find it easy to adapt to new situations. However new circumstances may be forced upon him consequent upon death, disease or retirement, and limited psychotherapy with older people is often very rewarding. The novice may learn much from psychotherapy with such patients. Two precautions should be taken first however. First, the therapist should assure himself that the patient is not suffering from a psychotic illness (particularly an affective one). Second, he should satisfy himself about the state of his patient's physical health. He should make a careful initial physical examination, so that physical complaints are not dismissed as psychogenic without good reason. It is wise to confirm that the patient's previous personality has been a reasonably stable one. People who have lived their lives as neurotic semi-invalids do not improve as they get older.

The distinction between 'young' and 'old' patients begs the definition of the words 'young' and 'old'. Perhaps this is best considered in comparison to the age of the therapist. When patient and therapist are separated by two or more generations, the therapist should consider carefully whether he may be 'too old' or 'too young' to undertake the case.

Other factors

The therapist should not undertake therapy with someone to whom he takes a profound dislike or of someone whom he finds excessively attractive. In such cases he would be better to ask someone else to treat the patient, and he should examine his own personality in an attempt to discover why he feels as he does (see counter-transference p. 64).

He should never undertake therapy with patients who are being treated by someone else. If he discovers fortuitously that the patient is attending another therapist, he should proceed no further. The patient may protest that he likes his present therapist better, or that the other therapist does not understand him. There may be other indications of disharmony. The therapist should advise the patient to pass these facts on to the original therapist. It will be helpful if he writes to the other therapist, describing what has happened.

The therapist should not offer intensive psychotherapy to patients who are suffering from a psychotic illness. Such people usually respond very well to the appropriate medication, and whilst the doctor will show interest in them and will be willing to support them, he need not subject them to an analytic 'dissection'. It is said sometimes that is harmful to do so. This is not the author's experience, but he does not find it very fruitful and regards such analysis as a poor use of therapeutic time.

The therapist should not try to treat patients who have very serious personality disorders—people who are habitually dishonest, impulsive, irresponsible, and self-centred. Patients who regard themselves as uniquely lovable, or who think what a great privilege it must be to have the opportunity of 'treating' them, are unlikely to change.

It is not usually possible to alter the direction of sexual drive. Homosexuals cannot usually be changed, although, as Freud pointed out in a famous letter (p. 97) the therapist may be able to help them deal with some of the difficulties which stem from their deviation.

An inexperienced psychotherapist would be unwise to undertake psychotherapy when he is advised not to do so by someone whose opinion he respects. He should be wary of undertaking psychotherapy simply because he is asked to do so. The final decision as to whether or not a patient should be accepted for intensive psychotherapy by him is his, and his decision will depend on his own view of the case. Naturally he will take into account the views of others.

A therapist should not undertake psychotherapy with friends, relatives or neighbours. It is necessary for him to remain at a professional 'distance' from his patient and this is not possible when the two are closely acquainted. The therapist should not undertake the treatment of patients of whom he stands in awe. Neither should he undertake psychotherapy with someone, simply because he is flattered at being asked to do so.

If psychotherapy is to be successful the patient must be able to recognise and accept the contribution which he has made to the problem, and he must be willing to make the necessary alterations in his own behaviour. He must be prepared to pay more than lip service to the proposition that problems do not arise solely out of the regrettable behaviour of *other* people. He must be prepared to face the fact that there are some aspects of himself of which he is ignorant, and of which he would prefer to know nothing, but which must be examined nevertheless for the contribution which they make to the problem as a whole. The patient who regards himself as uniquely admirable and shamefully ill-used is not suitable for therapy.

It is much more easy to describe patients who should be rejected than those who should be accepted. The ideal patient is neither too old nor too young, and has made a reasonable adjustment to life. This is evidenced by his satisfactory work record and stable domestic relationship. He is almost certainly free of any criminal activity, and his problem has been precipitated by considerable trauma. He is reasonably intelligent, and is prepared to inconvenience himself to a considerable degree in order to obtain relief. He will already have made some attempt to overcome his problem for himself, and will truly understand that the problem will be resolved largely as a result of the efforts which he himself makes. He will be prepared to tolerate some discomfort. It will be seen, therefore, that ideal patients are those who are relatively 'healthy'.

Selection of the therapist

The first stage of selection is when the therapist chooses himself. He thinks 'I should like to be a psychiatrist' or 'I would like to be a marriage guidance counsellor'. When an interview is included in the formal selection procedure, he will be asked his reasons and he will usually respond with an innocent platitude about wishing to help other people—either because of his own supreme happiness, or because some devastating experience has given him an understanding which he would like to share with others.

The potential therapist must obviously give very serious consideration to his choice of career. What does he really expect from psychotherapy? In his heart he will know that there are many reasons including several selfish ones. He will, amongst other things, hope to obtain an understanding of his own mind, and his curiosity about the doings of other people will be amply rewarded. If, however, he has a serious personal problem which he has been unable to resolve, he will *NOT* find the solution by undertaking the therapy of others. Like the marriage guidance counsellor in Chapter I, he must put his own house in order before he attempts to help others.

If he is already a member of one of the helping professions, he will already have undergone a formidable period of training, and will have learned something of what may be expected of him. Further postgraduate study will be required before his training is completed, and he will have a number of obstacles to overcome before he is firmly established on his chosen career. He may fall by the wayside, in which case he may choose to blame the 'system', but the fault is more likely to be his own. He has embarked upon his career for the wrong reasons.

Individuals who wish to join one of the voluntary counselling organisations are usually subjected to an intensive series of interviews, case discussions, psychological tests and so on, which are designed to probe their suitability for the job. These organisations carry a very high degree of responsibility and public esteem, and they are rightly jealous of their voluntary status, so that their selection process may be even more strict than it is for the potential psychotherapist.

There is an obvious fascination in learning about how people work, about their private thoughts and shameful secrets. It is exciting—and often a little alarming—to discover how one works oneself. Many people embark upon the work with enormous enthusiasm and high hopes, but quickly find themselves demoralised and defeated. They may find their work more arduous and exacting than they had realised, or monotonous and sometimes frightening. Sometimes they feel that they are getting nowhere, and their mentors may have very little comprehensible guidance to offer.

It may happen that the therapist will be confronted with the most distressing experience he can suffer in his professional career—the death of a patient by his own hand. This may happen when suicide is the only solution that a patient can find for his problems. Some patients habitually use suicide attempts in order to mobilise their resources. Then one day something goes wrong, and they die.

From the start, the psychotherapist and the counsellor must face the fact that sometimes it will happen: that occasionally their patients or their clients will kill themselves. Sometimes they will give an advance warning of their intention, but sometimes they will give none. Occasionally, it is only in retrospect that the therapist will realise that a warning was given. Occasionally he will take a gamble that the threat will not be carried out—only to find that he was wrong. But whatever has gone before, if a patient kills himself, the therapist will always experience shock, distress and remorse. Suicide is distressing enough however it is encountered, and no one should undertake psychotherapy or counselling if he feels that he might be overwhelmed with remorse if it should occur. Even with the most careful precautions, it is not always possible to prevent such a happening. An experienced therapist may mistakenly recommend that the risk must be taken, in the patient's interest, and subsequently be shown to be at fault.

Of course, the therapist must be intellectually and physically mature. It is desirable that he should have successfully passed some of the major hurdles of life, such as marriage and parenthood. He should be fairly well on the road to his chosen career. He should have shown a reasonable degree of stability in both his work and his personal life. If he is married, his spouse will not object to his choice of career.

He should be free of any major personal problems, and there will be no problems at all which he cannot share with at least one other person. He must himself be free from any serious illness, whether physical or psychiatric. If he has had any form of nervous illness, the doctor who was responsible for his treatment should be willing to certify that he is now fully well. If it is considered necessary, the candidate should be willing to submit himself for an independent psychiatric opinion.

Counselling and psychotherapy should not be undertaken against the advice of objective advisers, such as doctors, ministers, etc., and the therapist should not have suffered a major change in his way of life in recent months. Someone who has been widowed recently is usually unsuitable.

Counselling and psychotherapy demand a very high degree of personal self-discipline and those who undertake it must aim for the highest degree of professionalism to which they are capable. It is unfair to their patients and clients that they should aim for anything less. The counsellor must have sufficient time for counselling. He should be prepared to complete a training programme which may last for two years or more, and should be willing to counsel for at least a further two years after his training has been completed.

There will be time when he is subjected to criticism, and sometimes this will not seem justified. He may hear harsh words from his clients, his teachers, or his fellow counsellors, and he must be willing to pay attention to them. He must be willing to modify his way of working when it seems that the criticisms are justified. When they are not justified, he should not feel the need to assert himself to such a degree that his critic is forced to retract.

He must recognise that by helping one person there will be occasions when he may hurt another. By pleasing one he may offend someone else. Naturally, he will aim to help as many people as possible, but it is seldom that everyone is pleased. Some people will condemn him to his face, but others will condemn him behind his back, and he may only hear about such criticisms in a roundabout way. Sometimes he will not hear them at all.

His good intentions may be condemned from unexpected quarters. It may be possible to fool *all* of the people for some of the time: it is certainly not possible to *please* them all, even for some of the time. There is a fairy story for grown-ups by Anthony Armstrong entitled 'The Prince who Hiccupped'. In order to break a magic spell, a king had to perform a deed which would bring him the gratitude of everyone in the land. He decided to organise a birthday feast, in the course of which wine would flow free, in every fountain in the land. He supposed that this would bring the thanks of everyone. But instead of receiving universal gratitude he was immediately greeted with a series of complaints:

about the disorganisation of their service, from the Water Supply Company;

about the small number of fountains in farming areas, by the agricultural and labourers union;

about the quality of wine supplied;

about the quantity of wine supplied;

about there being wine at all from the representatives of fifteen temperance organisations.

The Patient's Expectations

When a patient comes for therapy, it is usually with a fairly confident expectation that his problem will be solved simply and fairly painlessly. He supposes that the therapist, like Sherlock Holmes, will be familiar with similar cases from the past, either from his own experience or from that of other people. Indeed, these expectations may lead him to complain that the therapist is trying to pigeon-hole him, rather than to treat him as a unique human being.

He will certainly expect the therapist to tell him what to do, to provide a few simple instructions whereby his difficulty may be resolved, and to tell him what is wrong with his own behaviour so that he can make the appropriate changes. He may often express himself very willing to accept criticism. But the therapist may find little to criticise, because the problem lies between the patient and someone else, not between the patient and the therapist. The account which he gives may appear to be very reasonable, and the complaints which he makes about the behaviour of others entirely justified.

The newly fledged therapist will often share the patient's fantasy that he can tell him what to do, and in consequence he may often make too many suggestions. But even as he does so, the therapist will perceive how valueless they are, and how little impression they make on the patient. After all, it is probable that he has considered them all and dismissed them himself.

The patient will certainly hope for a very rapid solution to his problem. He will not realise that many sessions will be required and that these will often seem repetitive and unproductive. There will be times when he will question his wisdom in having undertaken therapy. If one problem is resolved, it may reveal others, even more confusing and alarming. Most patients persist nevertheless. They accept the rules of therapy, its reservations and its disadvantages. They know that the risk of failure is sometimes the price of success. Although they may suffer anguish and distress, they will, if they have a mind to, learn to make the most of their assets, and to find a fuller life despite all difficulties.

The 'contract'

At this point it is appropriate to consider what the therapist expects of his patient and what the patient may expect of the therapist: in other words, to examine the 'contract' which exists between them.

The contract is, of course, an unwritten one, and it is largely unspoken. It is based on a mutual understanding that the patient seeks that assistance which the therapist believes to be most appropriate. Their relationship is a professional one, never a social one, and the contract helps to define its limits in those few cases in which they are not clear.

The therapist requires of the patient that during the sessions he will endeavour to put into words all that he thinks and feels. At no time may he touch the therapist. He may laugh or cry or he may express his emotions in words. He may not lie to the therapist, no matter how good his intentions may be. He will not drink alcohol on the day of the session. He will arrive at the correct time and will leave when told to do so by the therapist.

For his part the therapist will attend to all that he hears, however disagreeable it may be, and whether it is disgraceful, offensive, personal, or disloyal. He will neither praise nor criticise the patient. The information he is given will belong to the organisation to which the therapist belongs. Confidentiality will only be breached in quite exceptional circumstances. (Such a case may occur if the therapist is ordered to do so by a Court.) The therapist makes no promises to his patient. He gives no guarantee that the problem will be solved, or that the patient will benefit by his attendance.

Occasionally the patient may break these rules, although there is no reason for the therapist to do so. When the patient's behaviour exceeds the bounds of the contract, he should be told that it is unacceptable. If he persistently disobeys the rules, the therapist must discuss with him whether or not therapy can continue.

It cannot continue if the limits are disregarded. If, despite adequate warning, the patient persists in disobeying the rules, therapy must be terminated. In cases in which this final sanction is imposed—it is rarely required—the therapist will not resume therapy with the same patient at any time in the future. This is because the therapist must never allow himself to be cajoled into departing from his promise. Patients expect promises to be kept.

3. What does the Therapist do?

CARDINAL PRINCIPLE: Verbalisation precedes resolution.

In fictional psychiatry there are three characters: the psychiatrist, middle-aged and dark eyed, with a soupcon of accent and a secret sorrow; a handsome young assistant—a sort of latter-day Rudolph Valentino—a combination of detective, foil and man-about-town; and the patient—blonde, capricious, sinful; beginning to see the error of her ways and anxious to reform. The patient lies on the couch, the lights are dimmed and she tells of her childhood and her sex life, whilst the psychiatrist looks gravely on. Later he plays back a tape recording of the session to his handsome young assistant, and tells him to take her out to dinner. The sight of a child, crying in the street, reminds the patient that when she was three years old her doll was taken away from her. In the last scene, and for reasons which are apparent only to him, the psychiatrist tells her that this is the cause of her troubles, whereupon her symptoms disappear and she marries the handsome young assistant.

The reader will not be surprised to learn that this deviates from what actually happens in a number of respects. First, there is no handsome young assistant. Patients are rarely beautiful. No-one takes anyone out to dinner (the patient may issue an invitation, but the therapist may never accept—see later; 'the transference'). No-one marries anyone. There is not necessarily a couch, and the lights are never dimmed. Most important of all, the therapist does not chance upon a single incident which explains the whole problem, and leads to instant and total cure.

Since many readers will have only this sort of fictional model to guide them, it is necessary to discuss, in some detail, just what it is that the therapist does and does not do.

When a patient comes for psychotherapy, and when all extraneous material is eliminated, he says, essentially, 'I have a problem. It must be solved. Tell me what to do'. The first thing that the therapist must understand is that neither he nor anyone else can *tell* the patient what to do. This is obvious to both patient and therapist. But neither does the therapist advise the patient or suggest what to do. This may be rather surprising. After all, surely the patient is coming to obtain suggestions and advice?

This is probably true—at first, anyway, but the therapist is not an adviser. If he were, he might be replaced by a comprehensive memory-store in due course, operated by a computer. All the data would be fed in, and the solution obtained painlessly within seconds. Like Sherlock Holmes the computer would be able to say, 'You will find similar cases on such and such a dare'.

For *advice* to be of value, every circumstance of the problem must be known. The only person who can really know everything about the patient, is the patient himself. It would take a lifetime for him to tell it to someone else. Furthermore it is most unlikely that the patient would have reached the stage of consulting someone if the suggestions which a therapist could make have not been considered and rejected already. So the therapist does *not* give advice.

This raises a problem for the patient, for initially he has come for advice. Problems always arise between people. In this instance, the problem lies between the patient and his therapist. If the problem is not resolved, psychotherapy cannot continue. The solution is not an easy one. The patient is bound to accept that the therapist cannot *advise* him what to do. The solution can found only from within the patient's own resources. This is a puzzling conclusion for the patient, because hitherto he has been unable to find such an answer. The therapist offers the hope that the patient will come upon a solution as a result of their interaction. This is quite different from being told the solution. This conclusion is a 'painful' one, but problems cannot be solved without some degree of discomfort, both for the patient, and also for the therapist, who has to share the patient's disappointment that his original expectations will not be fulfilled. It would be pleasant for the patient, and gratifying for the therapist, if his problems could be overcome for him. But just as no-one can learn the piano for someone else, or win a race for someone else, or earn a living for someone else, or fall in love for someone else, no-one can overcome difficulties for someone else.

If then the therapist does not advise, what does he do? Does he reassure? Does he say 'I think things will come right' or 'I don't think you need have any fear of that' or 'that sort of thing almost never happens'? Well, he could reassure, but what purpose would such reassurance serve? Can he *know* that things will come right? Can he be *certain* that the patient need have no fear about that? Can he be *sure* that this is not one of those cases in which that sort of thing happens? Statistics do not reassure individuals. It is of no comfort to the relatives that the death of their loved one was caused by a million to one chance. Reassurance seldom reassures. Instead, the psychotherapist may go to the opposite extreme. Instead of assuring the patient that such an event is unlikely to happen, he will explore with him what it would be like if it did happen. How would things be if the worst were to happen? In other words, he will help the patient to see and to plan, even for remote possibilities. He will not assert that they will never happen.

If the therapist does not advise or reassure, does he explain? Does he explain that sometimes, when people are frightened, there is an increased amount of adrenalin in the bloodstream, and in consequence the heart beats faster, and sometimes it can be felt as a thumping in the chest, but that does not mean that the heart is diseased—in fact, rather the reverse. And that he can understand that the patient would be afraid when her husband threatens to strike her. Some men are simply like that, and after all she knew he was like that before she married him. And that marriage very seldom changes people for the better. And so on and so on. At the end of a long and rambling explanation such as this, the therapist is likely to be greeted with the question, 'Do you mean that I have heart disease doctor'? Explanation further confuses the patient; offers him new opportunities for hypochondriacal preoccupation; new opportunities of avoiding an examination of the core of the problem; of evading an examination of the relationship with significant people; of the pathology of the relationship out of which the problem has arisen.

If the therapist does not advise or reassure or explain, does he *encourage*? Does he say 'The trouble with you is that you think too much about yourself. Now, why don't you get yourself an interest? I used to be just like you. Then I took up golf. Why don't you do the same? You can join a golf club and meet a lot of nice people and get plenty of fresh air and exercise. That's what you want, plenty of fresh air and exercise. Why don't you try it?'

This approach is particularly favoured by those who describe themselves as 'A bit of a psychologist myself'—a claim made by 98 per cent of the general population and (when it suits them) 100 per cent of the medical profession. But for the patient, the problem is that to take up golf, for example, is precisely what he would like to be able to do. The reason for his coming to therapy is that he has been unable to do it. The ability to follow a suggested regime signals his cure: it is not the means by which the cure is achieved. One might just as well encourage a patient with chronic bronchitis to stop coughing. The therapist does not encourage.

The Therapist's Role

The first thing that the therapist offers a patient is his undivided, uncritical attention. He *attends* to everything that the patient does and says. He shares his observations with his patient. He sees, and tries to help the patient see, he hears and tries to tell the patient what he hears. He smells, he feels, he observes and all the time he shares.

His attention is a questioning one, seeking always to differentiate that which is deeply felt from that which is merely stereotyped convention. The therapist attends, not in the manner of a friend, who will ignore certain remarks and allow others to pass, nor in the manner of a foe, who seizes on anything that can be used to humiliate, condemn, or destroy. His attention is objective and dispassionate, free as far as possible, from preconceptions and prejudice. He tries to attend to what is there, rather than what he wishes to be there. If the relationship between therapist and patient were a social one, certain conventions would be tacitly acknowledged. It would, for example, be agreed that people do not have incestuous feelings for their close blood relatives, or hate their parents. In a social relationship it might be 'agreed' (with an downstage leer) that married men never look at other women. In a social exchange, one speaker may withdraw something which he has said, if it proves offensive to the other: he may offer an apology, which he expects to nullify the offence. The other will be expected to accept the apology, even though it fails in its purpose, and even though he may suspect the speaker of insincerity.

Social conventions have little part to play in psychotherapy. It is always assumed that whatever he says or does the patient means it. There is nothing so absurd that it can be dismissed without consideration. Behaviour cannot be modified retrospectively by a word of apology or a withdrawal.

'Paying attention' may seem a simple and modest requirement, but it is very much more difficult to achieve than the novice will realise. Even if he is forewarned of a trap, his attention may wander: he may be inclined to think that something is so obvious that it would be ludicrous to question it. An example which will be familiar to some readers is given below. A short phrase is enclosed within a triangle and the reader is asked to say what it is.

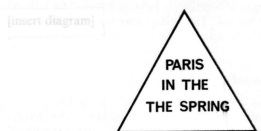

The *wrong* answer is given at the foot of page 31.

If the reader is familiar with this example, he may remember how easily he was caught at first, and he may still be astonished at the ease with which people fall into the trap, if they are not familiar with it.

The therapist listens to all the patient says, attends to all that he does, takes notice of every aspect of his behaviour, however trivial. Sometimes this is to the patient's considerable irritation. He may complain that his therapist makes no allowance for human frailty, and treats him more like an an object under a microscope than a human being. He will complain that he can neither say—nor do—anything which is not subjected to detailed examination.

To some extent this is true, although behind these complaints the reader will recognise a demand that the therapist should be less exacting, less observant and less professional in his approach. The therapist would like to please his patient, but he knows that he cannot be too professional if he is to be of help. His technique may not be modified simply because the patient finds it uncomfortable, for without some degree of discomfort, no change is to be anticipated.

The new therapist will wonder about attending; about listening and observing; and will wonder how such a simple exercise can be of any value. He will question the value of 'just talking' or 'just listening'. How can mere words do any good? The power of words must never be disparaged. Words may raise the lover, for example, to the heights of ecstatic anticipation, or to the depths of despair.

The act of giving the patient his full attention is far more arduous and fatiguing than the reader will realise. Nothing must escape his attention. Does the patient come late or early, or is he on time? How is he dressed? How does he open the session? How does he continue? What does he remember? What does he forget? The therapist is searching for one or two themes: themes which will be repeated throughout the session, themes which will be perceived eventually as recurring throughout the patient's life. Each piece of his behaviour is part of the theme. The object is to complete a psychological jigsaw. There may be missing pieces, but if the correct pattern has been found, there will never be an extraneous one. As the therapist perceives the development of a theme, he endeavours to show it to the patient, to demonstrate how the pieces fit together, to help the patient find hitherto undiscovered pieces for himself. The patient may not be familiar with the total picture—indeed its unfamiliarity is often the reason for the problem having arisen.

Latent and Manifest Content

Nothing which is said or done may be dismissed as being of no significance. There are no mistakes, no errors, no slips of the tongue. The patient's protest that 'I didn't really mean that' is never accepted. Everything is examined for its underlying meaning. The underlying meaning of a communication is called its *latent content* whilst the communication itself represents the *manifest content*. The translation from manifest to latent content is called *interpretation*, and usually leads to some sort of emotional response on the patient's part. The response may be a flash of realisation—the 'aha' reaction; or one of indignation; one of questioning; of doubt; of sadness; perhaps of pallor or blushing. The therapist must beware the interpretation which merely produces good natured or compliant agreement, with no emotional response whatsoever, or one of only mild interest or mild disinterest.

Here is an example of what may happen when the therapist pays close attention to what a patient says. A man was talking to the doctor about his difficulties with his wife. He said 'I don't understand it. I love her. I try to be attentive to her. I am unfaith...faithful...to her'. When the last sentence was repeated to him he protested that it was just a slip of the tongue. It was a mistake; and had no significance. The doctor insisted that the husband had told him two contradictory things about his attitude towards his wife. The husband became very angry 'Of course I am not faith...unfaithful to her' he protested, and became even more angry when he realised he had repeated his slip of the tongue.

The *manifest* content of the communication was what the husband had tried to convey, and which hd did twice say—that he had been faithful to his wife. The *latent* content was the unintended statement that he had been unfaithful to her. The interpretation, that he had in fact been unfaithful, was to be confirmed much later.

Sharing

Now let us look at a case in which a counsellor shares his observations with his client. It is a very simple example and calls for no very deep understanding. There may be something to be learned from it nevertheless.

A client consulted a counsellor for the very first time. The first thing that the counsellor observed, before a word was spoken, was that the client had a bad smell. It was the sort of smell about which people are not told, even by their best friends. (To tell the truth such people rarely have best friends.) The client's complaint was that he had difficulty in getting on with people. At least part of the reason for this was immediately obvious to the counsellor, and it seemed astonishing that it was not also obvious to the client. Yet smell is something to which people very quickly become accustomed. They cease to notice it. The 'hospital smell', so familiar to patients is usually unrecognised by the staff. The boiled-cabbage smell of a boarding house may be remarked by everyone except the proprietor. The 'gasworks smell' may be indignantly denied by the local residents. So not only may a personal 'bad smell' pass unnoticed, it may be repudiated by the offender.

The client's olfactory sense was anaesthetised to his own offensive odour, and it was the counsellor's difficult task to awaken the client from his anaesthesia. Clients may be blind to facts which are startlingly obvious to others. Unless the counsellor had been prepared to share his observations with his client, he could do nothing to help him overcome this first obstacle to getting on with people. It is often difficult

See p. 29.
The wrong answer is 'Paris in the Spring'. If the reader persists in getting the incorrect answer he should make an exact copy of the diagram.

and embarrassing for the counsellor, and the client may be hurt, offended, even very angry, but there is no way in which he could be given such information without suffering distress.

The 'insights' which are given in therapy frequently cause pain and this is unavoidable. It is the experience of pain which leads the patient to change his behaviour in a constructive way. The therapist cannot help his patient effectively if he is unwilling to cause him pain.

In the example quoted, note that the counsellor did not *tell* the client what to do. He did not even advise him what to do. He certainly did not reassure him that his impact on other people was clean and in-offensive. He did not offer—or accept—any 'rational' explanation of the offence ('I haven't been too well lately and when I'm not well I often develop a slightly sweaty smell. I have been to my doctor about it...he gave me some lotion to use.') The counsellor attends to his client and shares his observation with him. He leaves the client to decide whether to accept the observation and whether to do anything about it.

Verbalisation

The therapist can share his observations with his patient only if he puts them into words. Similarly the patient can convey his problems to the therapist only by verbalising them. Verbalisation precedes resolution. Not infrequently, and rather surprisingly, the act of putting a problem into words leads to its solution. This sometimes seems like magic, and the reader may wish to consider why it should be so.

Insight

The process of learning about one's personal mode of operation; the development of self-awareness; the understanding of how other people see one, is called insight. It is often a disconcerting experience. Over the years, each individual builds up a private picture of himself, what he looks like, what he sounds like, what his strengths and weaknesses are, what he can reveal to other people and what he must conceal from them. However, the picture is a distorted one. The physical image which the patient recognises as his own is strangely different from that which is familiar to others, for it is the reflection that he sees in the mirror. It is often difficult to find a photograph which pleases the subject, because although the camera cannot lie, the mirror can. There are very few who find the recorded sound of their own voice a pleasant experience. More often, it is an unrecognisable horror, grossly distorted (one hopes) and full of technical deficiencies. Yet this is the voice which, over the years, others come to accept, to like and sometimes to love.

Individuals resist insight, preferring to believe in their own distorted views of themselves, and often rejecting with indignation anything that conflicts with their own. Thus, in 'Pygmalion' the irascible, impatient, intolerant, Professor Higgins is asked by his housekeeper not to use a certain, most improper word beginning with 'b'. (The play was written in 1912.) Higgins protests loftily that 'I cannot charge myself with having ever uttered it, Mrs Pearce. Except perhaps in a moment of extreme and justifiable excitement'. His housekeeper replies 'Only this morning, Sir, you applied it to your boots, to the butter and to the brown bread'. Higgins retorts 'Oh that! Mere alliteration, Mrs Pearce, natural to a poet'. Later he confides to his companion 'You know, Pickering, that woman has the most extraordinary ideas about me. Here I am, a shy, diffident, sort of man. I've never been able to feel really grown-up and tremendous, like other chaps. And yet she's firmly persuaded that I'm an arbitrary over-bearing bossing kind of person. I can't account for it'. And he really can't. He has no insight whatsoever.

4.   What does the Therapist say?

CARDINAL PRINCIPLE: Everything has a meaning.

The repeated experience of Dr Kildare was that he did not really have to say anything. Sometimes, if he did say something, the patient's attention was diverted from its goal. When this happened, his intervention was more of a hindrance than a help.

The first rule then, is that if the therapist has nothing to say, he should say nothing. There is no value in talking simply to keep the conversation going. Time and contemplation are required in psychotherapy and solutions to problems emerge only slowly. The instant solution, so much a characteristic of fictional psychiatry, is to be regarded in actual practice with great suspicion.

Nevertheless, there are many occasions on which the therapist will wish to speak, and here we must discuss briefly the reasons for this, when so much can be achieved simply by listening.

The first reason, of course, is that the relationship between the patient and therapist is one between two people, and effective communication between them demands an *exchange of words.* The relationship is a professional one, not a social one, and it has a very specific purpose. This is to facilitate that activity which is therapeutic for the patient: that of the communication to his therapist of his thoughts and feelings, and to assist the recall of half-forgotten memories, which may lead to further meaningful elaboration of current thoughts and feelings.

If *facilitation* is the first purpose of the therapist's share of the exchange, the second is *clarification.* This is necessary to enable the therapist to facilitate effectively. In order to help the patient understand, the therapist must himself understand. His understanding is often only a fraction ahead of the patient's. When he asks for clarification, the content may become clarified for the patient.

It has already been noted that everything must be examined for its latent meaning. An example is given by a patient who described how, on one occasion some years previously, she had promised to take her mother shopping for a birthday present. She was looking forward to this outing, but when she called at the house, she found to her dismay that her mother was out, and there was no message. The patient had travelled some distance, so she scribbled a note and returned home. Next day her mother telephoned. 'You were supposed to come on

Thursday' she said. 'That's right' said the patient 'why weren't you there?' An argument developed, and the patient found herself on a quite different wavelength from her mother. Then, suddenly, she realised that yesterday was *Friday*, and that she should have called the day before. She passed the whole thing off with a laugh. 'It must have been my unconscious, playing me tricks' she said. The therapist was very interested in this story and made an interpretation. 'It sounds as though you didn't want to buy your mother a present' he said. The patient was highly indignant. 'What a terrible thing to say' she cried, bursting into tears. 'I loved my mother very much. If you had any idea of how much I miss her, you wouldn't say things like that'. The therapist was intrigued by the patient's response and by her angry denial of his interpretation. In due course he was to obtain evidence that it was true. The patient was very hostile indeed towards her mother, but her hostility was quite unconscious. In consequence she herself failed to recognise it, and her hostility was displaced from the mother to the therapist.

Unconscious motivations

The problem arises of how it can happen that certain attitudes may exist without the patient's being consciously aware of them. The answer lies in the concept of the *unconscious*. This proposition will be examined more fully in Chapter 5, but here it is sufficient to note that those thoughts and feelings, ideas and wishes which are socially 'wrong' are made *unconscious*. The patient who said jokingly that 'It must have been my unconscious playing me tricks' was indicating that the real significance of her mistake was too painful for her even to consider. If a 'discreditable' unconscious motive is discovered, the patient is unlikely to receive it with enthusiasm. Instead the therapist may be astonished at the vehemence with which it is rejected.

The therapist offers first an attending ear, then, if possible, also an understanding ear. The understanding ear endeavours to be objective. It attempts to understand what is really happening, not what the patient would like to think is happening. It understands in another sense too. It appreciates that 'understanding' is at times difficult, painful, frightening, disconcerting, or embarrassing to the patient, and it understands that because of these responses, the patient will often wish that the objective truth is other than it is.

Asking questions

It is more important for the therapist to listen to the patient than for the patient to listen to the therapist, but there are occasions when the therapist must put questions. He will wish to question the patient if he has failed to understand what is being said, or when a new topic about which he knows little or nothing is embarked upon. He will wish to question a patient who seems to be having difficulty in speaking about a topic, or who appears to be evading it.

Questions should be as brief as possible, and should be phrased in such a way that they are easily comprehended. They should ask only one question, and should be pruned of extraneous matter ('sort of thing', 'if you follow me', 'or what', 'as it were', 'and so on'). Technical terms should be avoided.

Sometimes the therapist will find that he has phrased a question badly, or that he has asked one which he did not really intend. He may then be tempted to rephrase the question in the way originally intended. However it is better to allow the patient to answer the 'wrong' question. Sometimes this provides unexpectedly useful information. The 'right' question can be put when the 'wrong' question has been answered. Sometimes the patient will answer the 'right' question when the 'wrong' one has been put.

The therapist must beware of suggesting the answer to his questions. An inexperienced therapist asked correctly, 'How did you get on with your mother?' There was a pause, and the therapist added, 'I mean, did you get on well with her, or badly, or was she possessive, or did she let you do what you liked, or what?' The patient felt that he should reply with one of those four responses, when none really fitted the case. The patient may take a very long time to marshal his thoughts, and the therapist must wait patiently for the answer, thereby acknowledging that time and contemplation are required before problems can be solved.

Questions may be 'specific' or 'open-ended'. Open-ended questions are usually of more value. In them the question is phrased in such a way, that the answer demands *more* than a simple monosyllable. The 'open-ended' question may lead to fruitful elaboration. The question 'Do you get on well with your mother?' requires only a 'yes' or 'no' answer. It is much more useful to ask, 'How do you get on with your mother?' The answer should always be attended to very carefully, for it may be evasive. One patient, when asked how she got on with her mother replied, 'Mother was a wonderful person. She would do anything for anyone. She always had a kind word for strangers. Everyone loved her. There were more than 200 people at her funeral'. The therapist had to point out that the question had not been answered, and it transpired that the relationship had been very bad indeed.

'Specific' questions require a factual answer, such as 'yes', 'no', 'in 1960', and so on. They may require the patient to make a commitment or a decision. The patient may be asked when he was born, if he wishes to continue with therapy knowing the difficulties it involves, or whether he has any sexual problems. Specific questions should always be used sparingly, especially in matters involving personal and intimate details. Sometimes, when the patient is still new to therapy and uncertain of his therapist, he may be trapped into telling a later-to-be-regretted lie. He may be asked, for example, 'Do you have any sexual problems?' but be ashamed or reluctant to confess that he has. In consequence he may give an untrue answer. This sort of situation can be avoided by phrasing the question in a slightly different way. He may be asked, 'Do you have any sexual difficulties *about which you wish to talk with me*?' If the answer is 'yes' the patient may be asked to proceed. If it is 'no' the answer is a *reserved* one.

The therapist should take note of *reserved* answers, for they leave the primary question open. He will need to remember them because later the patient may protest that the answer he gave was a reserved one. If a patient is asked a question about feelings, such as 'Do you ever feel violent?' and his reply is, for example, 'generally speaking, no' he has given a reserved answer.

Inaudible questions

If the patient does not hear a question, he will usually ask the therapist to repeat it—unless he is too frightened or over-awed to do so. When this happens, the therapist should repeat the question in a louder tone of voice, using as far as possible the same words. He should *not* rephrase it. The patient may not have heard the *words* of the question but he has probably caught the cadence and the rhythm. If the question is rephrased, the 'tune' is changed and the patient may be confused. He is not prepared for a 'new' question and may feel that in missing the 'old' one, he has been deprived of something of importance.

Interruptions

Wherever possible the patient must be allowed to tell his story without interruption. There are nevertheless certain circumstances in which an interruption is necessary. For example, the patient may be in full flow and time is running out. He must be interrupted at a convenient point and told how much time there is remaining to him. Sometimes the patient will interrupt the therapist. The therapist should always allow the interruption to take precedence: afterwards he can repeat what he was saying.

Participants in joint interviews (q.v.) should be discouraged from interrupting each other. If one has an objection to make, he may be assured that he will be given an opportunity of putting it when his partner has concluded.

Talking 'over' a patient—forcing views on him whilst he is trying to express his—is usually an expression of a negative counter-transference (q.v.). The therapist should examine his own motives.

Cadence and stress

We sometimes mock the Chinese for using the same word to mean 'yes' and 'no'. We think of it as an absurd contradiction. But we ourselves may use a phrase which takes on opposite meanings, according to the way in which it is stressed. When this happens, a communication may take on a completely new significance. For example, a family was looking forward to a picnic, but the day was dull and windy, it was wet and cold, and everything seemed to go wrong. 'This is a fine day for a picnic' they grumbled. The next day was bright and warm. The sun was shining and there was a gentle breeze. The skies were blue and the birds were singing. 'This is a *fine* day for a picnic' they exclaimed. The father, who did not like picnics, muttered to himself 'This is a bloody awful day for a picnic'. A patient may make a slip, not of the tongue, but of the *tone*, and it is necessary to adhere to the tone as closely as possible when the therapist reflects a slip to him.

Answering questions

The therapist should not be in too great a hurry to answer questions. He must first consider what may lie behind the question. What relevance does it have to the present stage of therapy. He must ask himself whether the patient is seeking the answer to a fact (in which case, he could find the answer from the same sources as are available to the therapist), or for advice, reassurance, etc. In each case the therapist must wonder why the patient seeks advice, or reassurance? Sometimes he seeks an opinion, but the reader is reminded that matters of opinion, based on experience of similar cases, may have little to do with an individual's case, which is always unique.

The standard and rather stereotyped way of responding to questions is 'What are your thoughts about it' or 'Why do you ask that'. A variant of these forms of reply is usually the best.

Sometimes, when a question is asked, it is helpful for the therapist to try to imagine himself to be in the patient's shoes: and to wonder what might have given rise to the question. This occasionally provides an explanation.

For example, a patient in a medical ward, who had been investigated for two or three days for symptoms suggestive of intestinal disease, asked the nurse whether the results always took a long time to come. The nurse was tempted to 'reassure' the patient that they required expert examination and interpretation, but that they would be completed as quickly as possible. Instead, she remembered to put herself in the patient's shoes, and replied 'It must seem that you have been waiting an eternity'. The patient burst into tears and cried for the rest of the day. Her father had died of cancer of the stomach and she was sure the same fate awaited her. The expression of her fear and the accompanying grief had a remarkable effect. The next day her symptoms had disappeared completely, and although several days elapsed before the tests were completed, her symptoms, her fear and her apprehension had quite gone. The fact that the test results were negative, was pleasing to hear, but the reassurance was no longer necessary.

The new therapist should be as sparing as possible in giving replies to questions. He must be on the alert for things which are not as they seem to be. He must free his mind from prejudice and preconceptions, and be especially wary of anything which seems unduly obvious.

Abreaction

Quite frequently the therapist will comment on what the patient has said. Such comments may be made to facilitate further communication, or represent an endeavour to understand the latent meaning of the communication.

Sometimes, having spoken a few sentences, the patient will pause and appear to be thinking. The therapist may help him to put his thoughts into words, perhaps simply by repeating the last few words he spoke. At other times it may become apparent that the patient has fallen silent, because of the development of an emotion. The expression of emotion has a vital part to play in the understanding of a problem, and in its solution. Whenever an emotion is observed the patient must be encouraged to express or *abreact* it. The therapist may observe the trembling of the lips and the reddening of the face in grief; the flush of embarrassment, the glaring eyes and pale skin of anger. In each case he may say 'It seems that the topic has caused you distress (or sadness or embarrassment or anger)'. The accuracy of the interpretation will usually be confirmed by a heightening of the emotion. If the therapist does not understand why the topic has had such an effect, he must ask. Abreaction of emotion is a very important procedure in psycho-therapy.

The non sequitur

The interpretation of the non sequitur provides some of the therapist's most spectacular work. He will be puzzled why a comment has been made, but should restrain himself from asking questions too quickly. Often the answer comes out of the blue, much later on, perhaps during a silence, or even after the session has been completed. Sometimes no answer is forthcoming. Some examples will be given of the interpretation of non sequiturs.

A patient was sent for a chest X-ray. On his return he commented that the machine seemed rather old-fashioned. The doctor deduced correctly that the patient had doubts about the reliability of the examination. He was certain that he had tuberculosis and the normal result did not reassure him.

Early in therapy a patient described how she had gazed at the dead body of her mother. 'She looked beautiful' she said. 'She looked 20 years younger. Her cheeks were pink. It was just as though she was asleep'. At a later session she repeated this description, almost in the same words. Then she asked the barely relevant question, 'Do undertakers use cosmetics on dead people?' The therapist was nonplussed for a moment, and was about to reply that he did not know, when suddenly the significance of the question came to him. If cosmetics had *not* been used, it might have been that the pink-cheeked mother was still alive. In failing to draw attention to this fact the patient would, therefore, have been responsible for burying her mother alive. This indeed was the daughter's fear, and she anticipated a similar fate in retribution. She had left very careful instructions in her Will that an artery should be opened before she was buried, but she did not trust her executors to carry out her wishes.

Another patient sent for the doctor when her father suddenly became very ill. The doctor did not come for two hours. 'Of course he is a very busy man' she excused him. The therapist took note of the excuse and asked what would have happened if the doctor had come sooner. The patient thought that her father would have survived. She blamed the doctor, and also herself, for not finding another doctor who might have come more quickly.

A wealthy businessman who had been charged with drunk driving was referred to a psychiatrist by his general practitioner, Dr Smith. It was considered that he was not motivated for treatment. The man was of considerable influence, and was rather taken aback when told that he would not be accepted as a patient. After he had assimilated the information he said to the psychiatrist, 'By the way I have an apology to make to you. Some months ago Jimmy Smith made an appointment for me to see you. I didn't keep it.' The patient assumed that he was being punished for failing to keep the appointment, although the psychiatrist had no knowledge that this had happened. By referring familiarly to 'Jimmy Smith', the patient indicated to the psychiatrist that he was on Christian name terms with the family doctor. Later it transpired that the man hoped to get his revenge on the psychiatrist by cutting off his supply of patients, at least from Dr Smith.

These specific examples are not of general value. They illustrate how the odd, irrelevant, paradoxical, superficial, communication may be found to have a significant latent meaning. They draw attention to some of the traps which await the unwary. They illustrate the importance of thinking about the inner meaning of a question, rather than searching for an answer to it.

The therapist need not ignore his intuition when helping the patient to say what is on his mind, for this may reflect the patient's total impact on him. Intuition is a curious thing but a very real one. It sometimes has a quality almost of telepathy, but telepathy is a 'para-normal' concept for which there is no room in psychotherapy. It probably arises from a rapid, mainly unconscious, summation of the impact which one individual makes on another. It comprises what he hears and sees of his companion: how he empathises with him: what his previous experience tells him. Sometimes his companion causes 'resonance' in his own unconscious.

It is a valuable but erratic asset in the psychotherapist, and may be misleading. Intuition should be used with great discretion and then not in terms of 'you feel' or 'I think you feel' but 'maybe you feel' or 'in similar circumstances some people would feel...'.

The therapist may be puzzled by an overtly irrelevant comment. He may be dimly aware that an apparent non sequitur may have more importance than appears on the surface. The patient may make a joke, yet in a curious way it is not a joke. Humour is irrelevant to therapy. The therapist should never make a joke at, with, or for, a patient, and if the patient makes one to him it should be examined seriously. It is useful to examine them in the light of 'true words are often spoken in jest'. Problems are not matters for joking, although in the social context, the joke is a useful device for softening hostile comments, introducing provocative ones, or of giving the hearer the choice of ignoring a topic or taking it seriously.

The patient may endeavour to impress the therapist by referring to his acquaintance with exalted personages. The underlying latent content of these remarks must always be explored.

The therapist must avoid appearing too clever. A patient was giving a garbled and increasingly confused account of an episode which occurred when she was 12 and, increasingly embarrassed said, 'You know what I am trying to say, don't you'. The therapist was new and unwary. He had a very good idea, but he did not know for sure. He played his hunch, 'It sounds as though you are trying to tell me that you became pregnant'. The patient was rather taken aback by what she saw as the therapist's almost telepathic perception. Thereafter, whenever she had anything difficult to say, she insisted that he knew what it was. Sometimes this was the case, but the therapist protested in vain that he did not *always* know.

It would be a great convenience, not only for the patient but also to himself, if the therapist were a mind-reader. It is sometimes tempting to accept that one possesses the gift of telepathy. However the therapist does not *know* what the patient is going to say until he says it. Furthermore, although saying 'it' may be difficult for the patient, it is one of several difficulties which must be overcome, and when he has learned to overcome one group of difficulties the patient may find it easier to overcome others.

Timing of the interpretation

An interpretation which is made prematurely runs a serious risk of being disregarded. Conversely if it is made too late its potential impact may be lost. The timing of an interpretation must be chosen with care. On the whole it is unwise to make an interpretation whilst the patient is already in the grip of a powerful emotion. It is better to wait until the emotion has been dissipated.

A patient became very angry indeed with his therapist. His anger seemed to be related to the frustrations that he had experienced with other men: his employer, his school-teacher, his elder brother and his father. The therapist tried to draw attention to these parallels but the patient became still more angry and left the room. At that moment his very considerable anger was directed towards the therapist. This made the therapist feel very uncomfortable, and he tried to deflect it to the source which (probably correctly) he perceived as the original one. In such circumstances as this it would have been better for the therapist to *accept* that the patient's anger was directed towards *him*. When this was done the patient's anger disappeared and then the therapist was able to discuss its original source with the patient. As he did so, the patient again became very angry: but now his anger was associated with a scene from the past which he remembered very vividly—when his father had favoured his elder brother.

Errors, lies and the truth

The problem of errors and slips of the tongue has already been considered briefly. The problem is to sometimes distinguish between the truth, what the patient sees as the truth, and falsehood. There is no way by which the 'truth' or 'falsehood' of a statement can be established. 'Truth drugs', and 'lie detectors', are fictions encouraged by liars, who wish to deceive the naive into believing in their sincerity.

The therapist may find himself doubting the patient's word and may sometimes catch him out in a piece of flagrant dishonesty. If this should occur persistently, the therapist must seriously consider whether he can continue to treat his patient.

Such dishonesty is rare. Once a patient has accepted the need for therapy, it should be assumed, in the absence of overwhelming evidence to the contrary, that he wishes to tell the truth, *as he sees it*. When such an error as a slip of the tongue occurs, or when for example, the patient forgets his appointment, the therapist should be willing to discuss fully with the patient the possible latent meanings of the mistake. It may be contrary to the truth as the patient sees it, but discussion may reveal that it is the truth. There is nothing so obvious that it can be accepted without question. Could it be that the patient did not wish to keep his appointment? Were things going badly? Was he growing tired—or perhaps alarmingly—was he growing too fond of his therapist? Were there things to be told, topics to be discussed, which the patient preferred to leave unsaid? Sometimes the patient will feel that errors may lead the therapist to think ill of him. This also needs to be discussed.

It is important that the therapist should not allow himself to be trapped into saying something that he himself does not really accept. He may be told that he has said or implied something that he does not believe. Often, he is unable to recall the precise occasion on which the topics was discussed, but if he is always true to himself, he can, if he wishes, truly reply 'That is not what I believe, and I do not think I would have said it'. On the other hand, if he ever connives in something that he does not truly accept, he will never be able to make such an assertion.

If a promise is made to a patient, it must be kept. The therapist must therefore be very careful about any commitment he may make. An adolescent boy was warned that if he continued to play truant from school, his adoptive father would be sent to prison. He continued to play truant, and was very angry when he came home to find that his father was still there.

Conventional and stereotyped phrases

The therapist should bear in mind that our culture has certain shared beliefs which are taken for granted. These conventional attitudes are held with a greater or lesser degree of sincerity. It can be said of very few married couples that they have never had a cross word; of very few husbands that they have never looked at another woman. If these assertions are made, the therapist will have little difficulty in questioning them. Other attitudes seem self-evident, and it may appear irrelevant, indeed almost impertinent, to question them. We assume, for example, that mothers love their children. For most mothers this is true, but it is not true for all, and if the therapist accepts such an assertion without question, he may miss something that lies at the heart of the patient's problem. Other conventional attitudes, which may not necessarily be correct, include, that people dislike going into hospital, particularly that they are afraid of mental hospitals, that they do not like taking drugs, or attending doctors, and that only psychiatrically ill people commit violent, sadistic, blood-thirsty, crimes. Little children are conventionally thought of being 'mild, obedient and good',* whereas they are often vicious, deceitful, spiteful, inquisitive and dishonest.

Generalisations

The therapist should always ask the patient for specific examples of a generalisation e.g. 'Sometimes I find myself getting rather irritated over nothing'. The therapist should always ask for an example.

*From 'Once in Royal David's City'.

Silence

From time to time the patient will lapse into silence. Silence is a method of 'communication', and may have many meanings. The significance should always be explored. It may be that the patient has become silent whilst he considers the therapist's interpretation and its implications. Such a silence is constructive and need not be interrupted. The patient may become silent when a new train of thought enters his mind. He may be silent out of deference to the therapist—especially in the earlier sessions. He waits for the therapist to tell him what to say.

He may become silent out of defiance. He feels hostile towards the therapist and his silence says 'It's about time you did something for a change—why should I do all the work'. When this occurs there may be an unspoken battle between the therapist and the patient, each wondering who will weaken first, each wondering who will be first to find the silence intolerable. Such a 'battle' is of no value to anyone, and the therapist should be wary of it. He need have no hesitation in breaking silences of this sort with an appropriate interpretation, repeated several times if necessary. The reason for the patient's desire to struggle with his therapist must be examined—and vice versa!

The patient may become silent for reasons of shame, disloyalty, and so on. It may be that he does not wish to convey his thoughts to the therapist. By remaining silent for these reasons he is breaking the original contract. The therapist must help the patient understand that such conscious resistance is not helpful in the therapeutic situation.

Doorstep communications

Not infrequently a patient may make an announcement of great moment, right at the very end of a session, sometimes just as he is about to leave the room. The significance of these 'doorstep communications' varies. They may be used as a means of prolonging the interview and in this case they should be interpreted as such. More often, and especially when they occur in earlier sessions, they may indicate that the patient has been unable to summon up sufficient courage to make his 'confession'. Time is slipping by, and unless he says it now, it will be too late. So some momentous announcement is made, sometimes one which provides an unexpected explanation of a problem which has been hitherto completely obscure.

Doorstep communications of this sort are too vital to be dealt with on the doorstep. Furthermore, it is often impossible to deal with it in the few remaining minutes of the interview. The therapist should not attempt to do either of these things. He should say 'What you have said seems to be of considerable importance. We cannot deal with it in the very short time that is left. Probably we will need a whole session. Will you remember to begin with it next time?'

'Next time' should, of course, be as soon as possible. The therapist should put the responsibility for raising the matter on to the patient's shoulders. He should ensure that the patient does what he is asked to do.

Recurrent themes

An important part of the therapist's work is to pick up and echo to his patient, themes which recur in the session. When this is done fruitful elaboration may follow. The recurring theme, which is often unconscious, may be indicated very early on in the session.

A patient was shown into the consulting room by the receptionist. He thanked her and said to the therapist 'What a nice girl that is'. He went on to apologise for being a few minutes late. He had had difficulty in finding a parking space and had been beaten to a place by a woman driver who cut in front of him.

The patient continued that there had been a problem in the office. One of his colleagues was carrying on an intrigue with a typist, and he was worried that the man's work was being affected. His own wife had been very angry when she had heard about it, and had ordered the patient to have nothing to do with the colleague. Then he recalled how during his courting days, his fiancee had once telephoned his mother to complain when he had gone out to a stag party.

A theme of troublesome, interfering females was interpreted by the therapist, and the patient then remembered how his sister had always angered him by playing the 'good little girl' in front of their parents, when both knew perfectly well that she was often the source of mischief for which he himself was punished. He felt that he could do nothing right in his mother's eyes and reacted with helpless resentment when she was angry with him. He loved her dearly but felt that he was always doomed to disappoint her. In his life, women were always good, loved but neglectful; or wicked, dishonest and plausible. He reacted as though they were always one or the other, and never considered the possibility that they might be anything else. His relations with women were complicated by such distorted perceptions, and his inability to make satisfactory relationships was based on these assumptions.

5. Some Psychological Mechanisms

CARDINAL PRINCIPLE: There is no Santa Claus.

In all cultures, some forms of behaviour are valued as being good, and others are condemned as bad. In our country. pride, lechery, envy, anger, convetousness, sloth and gluttony are bad, whilst charity and chastity, prudence, faith, modesty, felicity and honesty are good.

Appreciation of what is 'good' and what is 'bad' is learned early in life; mainly from the parents. They in turn learned it from their parents, and so on. The shared understanding of what is to be praised and what condemned gives the characteristic flavour to culture. What is 'good' in one culture may be 'bad' in another.

In Britain, for example, it is 'bad' for mothers and fathers to leave their children in the care of uncles and aunts, maybe for many years, whilst the parents work or study in another country. In other cultures, once called primitive, there is nothing wrong in this practice. After all, the children are loved and cared for by their own people, and they *know* that their parents love them.

The Conscience

The conscience is that part of the individual's personality which 'represents' his culture. It evaluates his behaviour according to its requirements and may have idiosyncratic qualities in addition. It does not prevent the individual from performing 'bad' acts but he may be discouraged from doing them by the knowledge that he will feel 'bad' if he indulges himself—even though he is never discovered. It is as though he would 'discover' himself, and experience shame and a fall in his self-esteem. When the conscience acts idiosyncratically, the individual feels 'bad' about behaviour that would not worry other people. An example is given by a young man who was oppressed because he had contributed to a farewell gift of wine glasses to a colleague. The young man believed that drink was evil, and he felt that he had done his colleague harm by contributing to the gift. If the individual does something which his conscience regards as 'good' he will feel 'good', even though no-one knows of his virtuous deed. He may contribute anonymously to a worthy cause, and enjoy a private glow of satisfaction.

The 'strength' of the conscience is a hypothetical concept. It appears that some people have 'strong' consciences and others have 'weak' ones. Some obey the law of the land to the uttermost letter, and would be burdened by the slightest deviation. They would no more drive at 32 miles per hour in a built-up area than take a toffee apple from a child. Others would take toffee apples from children without a thought. Most people have an 'average' conscience, which appears to be more concerned with individuals than with groups of individuals. They feel responsible towards their fellows individually, but not en bloc. To 'forget' to return money to an individual is 'bad'; to evade the payment of a debt to a government department is a matter for congratulation.

Problems arise for the individual when his understanding of what is 'good' and what is 'bad' is contradicted by demands of his body. For example, in a teetotal family a child may learn that alcohol is bad. But when he grows up he may find that he likes the taste and enjoys the effect. So he develops a sense of *guilt*. He endeavours to conceal his liking from the people whom he respects, on the assumption that they would be *ashamed* of him if they were to discover what was happening. *Guilt* is what an individual feels about his secret. *Shame* is what he feels when the secret is exposed. Neither are particularly pleasant emotions: the loss of a sense of being valued if shamed may lead an individual to keep his secret for as long as possible, even though he may carry an almost intolerable burden of guilt.

Defence Mechanisms

Let us consider some of the ways in which the individual may handle feelings about which he feels guilty.

In our culture, pregnancy outside marriage is evaluated as 'bad'*. A woman who becomes pregnant outside marriage invites the condemnation of others. She may try to undo what should never have been done, and seek a termination of her pregnancy. This too may invite disapproval: some will be angry that the 'criminal' has escaped the condemnation and shame which would have been her lot had she carried her child to term. On the other hand, she might continue her pregnancy. She might dispute boldly the convention that to be pregnant when unmarried is 'bad'. She refutes the convention defiantly and says that in these days it is not 'bad', it is 'good'. This is an example of *rationalisation*.

There are other ways of dealing with matters of which the culture may disapprove. To one is given the technical name of *denial*. The unmarried mother whose pregnancy is unwanted simply ignores the possibility that she may be pregnant. Her periods stop. Well, she has had a heavy cold. Heavy colds often cause her periods to stop. She begins to feel sick in the morning. She must have a touch of gastritis. She often gets gastritis with a heavy cold. She finds herself passing

*The author has heard of the Permissive Society.

more urine than before. Probably, the chill has gone to her bladder. Her breasts become heavy. She is getting fat, and must really go on a diet. Her abdomen begins to enlarge. She will certainly have to go on a diet. She feels kicking movements. Indigestion!

It may seem incredible that she does not realise that she is pregnant. But if pregnancy is 'bad', some mothers are unaware that they are pregnant until they go into labour. They are completely oblivious to something that is perfectly plain to everyone else.

Denial is a common psychological mechanism in normal people. It helps the individual to ignore completely any distasteful fact. If something unpleasant occurs, it is ignored. The assumption is that if no notice is taken, it will go away. We will meet denial again in our discussion on mourning (p. 103).

Another example of denial is provided by the case of a very intelligent lawyer who did extremely well at school. He gained a scholarship to his university, carried off all the prizes there, and climbed rapidly in his chosen profession. He knew nothing about his father. His mother said that he had died when the patient was a baby. He had seen no photographs of his father, and his mother never spoke about him, brushing aside any questions which he put to her. He was asked by an Insurance Company to supply a copy of his birth certificate but his mother declined to let him have it. Instead she offered to send it to the company on his behalf. The conclusion—that he was illegitimate—was immediately obvious to everyone but the patient himself. For him, illegitimacy was a slur on himself and a denigration of his mother. He would tolerate neither possibility. The possibility was denied.

All cultures have very strict rules about sexual behaviour. Nearly always, sexual activity with a blood relation is 'bad', as is a sexual relationship with a member of the same sex. The contemplation of either of these things is also 'bad'. If a man were to contemplate sexual activity with his mother or with his sister he would be 'bad'. In the event of such ideas coming to his mind, they are instantly *repressed*. Repression means forgotten beyond any possibility of recall.

Aggression is 'bad'. How can one deal with thwarted aggressive behaviour? Well, it may be used to *destroy* anything that has a taint of aggression! An aggressive individual may become a pacificist, and so demonstrate to the world that he is *not* aggressive. He may *fight* for the cause of pacificism, and gratify his aggressive drives in doing so! This is a device which both fulfils and repudiates the aggressive drive. It is called *reaction formation*.

Reaction formation may also be manifested by certain people who appear to be excessively puritanical. They go through the most innocent book with a fine tooth comb, searching for the *double entendre* or for any minor ambiguity which might affect public morality. They demonstrate to the world thereby their own purity, but by the same means they gratify their own unconscious prurience. The ultra-prude will read in A A Milne's 'When We Were Very Young':

>   John had
>   Great Big
>   Waterproof
>   Boots on;
>   John had a
>   Great Big
>   Waterproof
>   Hat;
>   John had a
>   Great Big
>   Waterproof
>   Mackintosh—
>   And that
>   (Said John)
>   Is That.

He will withhold this innocent verse from his children because his prurient mind concludes that John must be a rubber fetishist.

Another way of dealing with unwelcome feelings is to *displace* them from their real object to an indifferent one. Thus, dislike for the mother may be *displaced* on to the mother-in-law. This mechanism allows the mother to be wholly good but makes the mother-in-law wholly bad. It explains the popularity of hostile jokes against mothers-in-law.

Yet another method is called *projection*. The antagonism which is experienced *towards* a person is perceived as coming *from* him. The 'victim' now has a 'reason' for feeling antagonistic in return—although originally the antagonism emanated from him.

To hate one's parents and to wish them dead is 'bad'. But such feelings occur. In these circumstances the *thought* of their death may be *isolated* from the hate which induces it. The individual is consciously aware only of the thought, not of the feeling. The only *feeling* of which he is *consciously* aware is that of distress at the thought. The feeling of hate has been dealt with by *isolation*. In other cases, neither the hate nor even the thought is conscious, but an unformulated sense of guilt exists, and the individual endeavours to expiate his sense of guilt by a symbolic act which may be repeated many times. The guilt may make the individual feel 'dirty', so he washes his hands time and time again. But he does not feel clean, because he does not know what has made him feel dirty. This mechanism is known as *undoing*.

The psychological processes which have been described are called *defence mechanisms*. Each implies the existence of a thought, a feeling or a wish which is regarded as 'bad' by the individual. The mechanism allows him to turn his attention away from the 'bad' idea.

The Unconscious

The question arises, where does the 'bad' idea go. Apparently it does not cease to exist. The defence mechanism allows it to operate whilst the individual remains *consciously* unaware of it. The solution lies in the concept of the unconscious.

Thoughts and feelings, ideas and wishes, which are kept *unconscious* are not only *not* recognised consciously: they are rejected out of hand. Each individual's view of himself allows him to operate in his own culture with some degree of self-esteem. Attitudes which do not fit in with the requirements of the culture must be hidden. Not even the individual himself may recognise them, for their existence represents a threat to his security, to his view of himself, to his understanding of role in society and to its willingness to accept him. He is expected to conform to a set of rules which were originally laid down in the Bible He must honour his father and his mother, and not commit adultery. He must love his neighbours as himself. He must not steal, nor lie with his sister, nor curse the dead, nor put a stumbling block before the blind, nor prostitute his daughter (Exodus XX, Leviticus XIX XX).

It is easy to disobey most of these precepts, but difficult to disobey some. There is no reason why a man should not find himself sexually attracted towards his sister, except the non-logical one that 'she is my sister'. Consciously, at least, the precept is accepted without question. If there is any risk of its being disobeyed, the attraction is locked into the unconscious.

Those thoughts and feelings, ideas, and wishes which are kept *unconscious* are not only *not* recognised consciously; they are rejected out of hand, sometimes fiercely, sometimes with indifference, sometimes as plausible nonsense. They are seldom considered seriously. The unconscious remains unconscious. If a 'discreditable' unconscious motive is discovered, the patient is unlikely to receive it with enthusiasm, and the therapist may be astonished at the vehemence with which it is rejected.

The unconscious is a powerful weapon in the hands of those whose only desire in life is to be always right. A foolish therapist may make an interpretation: 'You hate your mother'. If the patient agrees, all is well. If he disagrees, the foolish therapist retorts, 'That is because it is in your unconscious'. Interpretation of the unconscious must be made with discretion. At the end of the day the only one who can really tell if the interpretation is correct is the patient himself. *Speculations* about unconscious content may be made from straws in the wind. Isolated clues must be noted, but interpretation should be reserved until the therapist can feel reasonably sure of his evidence.

Unconscious thoughts and feelings, wishes and ideas, do not lose their power: instead their confinement often seems to increase their strength. The individual resists all attempts to examine them. If they were released they might overwhelm *him*.

Resistance is encountered whenever there is a possibility that the content of the unconscious might be revealed. The doors are firmly closed, and it may be far too dangerous to open them. Resistance is sometimes conscious, but more often it is unconscious too. When resistence is conscious, the individual is aware of the thoughts that he does not wish to share with others. He refuses to discuss them with his therapist, sometimes from shame, at other times out of fear or loyalty. The patient who *consciously* resists sharing his thoughts with his therapist is breaking the original 'contract' (p. 25).

More often, resistance is unconscious. 'Something' prevents the patient from becoming aware of what is already unconscious, and the 'something' is itself unconscious. An endeavour must always be made to elucidate the nature of the resistance, to understand and interpret it. Verbalisation of resistance often leads to its resolution, and when this occurs, not only does the resistance become conscious, but also the unconscious thoughts which were being resisted. The uncovering and interpretation of resistance is therefore a vital part of psychotherapy.

What is it that impedes progress in this way? Sometimes an answer to this question may be suggested by the application of the 'principle of extremes'. What would be the *worst* thing that might happen to the patient if he were to follow through his thoughts? Might he murder someone? Might he start weeping and be unable to stop? Might he be so angry that he could never speak again? Might he have a heart attack and die? Might he go mad? Might he become a homosexual?

One patient dreamed that he was shaking hands with a friend. The friend insisted on calling himself 'Master Bates', which was the wrong name. The patient saw no significance in the name 'Master Bates', and none in the handshake. Later, he confessed the thing that he feared most in the world. It was that he might be a homosexual. At this point the significance of the dream became clear to him. He realised that it had a strong homosexual flavouring. He recognised that the name, Master Bates, was really a pun, and that the handshake symbolised physical contact between his friend and himself. Then he remembered that he was always very curious to hear about the sexual exploits of his friend.

The reader need not expect that interpretation is always greeted with an enthusiastic response. Instead he may find himself held to ridicule when he asserts that things might be other than what they seem. The *purpose* of a defence mechanism is to defend the individual who uses it. It allows him to think of himself as a wholesome and law-abiding citizen. It 'protects' him from insight. Any attempt to suggest that things are otherwise may be rejected out of hand, sometimes with scorn, sometimes with anger. The point will seldom be considered seriously.

When the therapist recognises a defence mechanism at work, he may first ask the patient to consider it as a proposition. Suppose that the patient is not as he thinks himself, almost excessively gentle, but on the contrary, quite overwhelmingly aggressive. What would it be like?

Dreams

Certain general statements be made about dreams. They are usually pictorial in form and it may be presumed that they are the consequence of mental activity. They sometimes tell a coherent story, but more often they are muddled and nonsensical. Sometimes they carry a considerable emotional charge, perhaps of pleasure, sometimes of fear. In the latter case, they are called nightmares. Sometimes they are surprisingly lacking in emotional tone. The dreamer may, for example, dream that he is walking down a busy road, quite naked, and yet quite unconcerned. They are often contradictory. They are usually forgotten very quickly, so that the dreamer finds his dream slipping away, even as he struggles to recall it. Psychotherapy is not concerned with magic, and dreams are therefore not to be regarded as means whereby the future can be foretold.

Freud believed that dreams represent the fulfilment of (usually) unconscious wishes. The wishes are unconscious, presumably because they are not acceptable to the conscious mind. In dreams, the wish may be disguised by conversion into allegorical form. If the transformation is successful, the wish is fulfilled, and the dreamer does not experience anxiety, so that the dream is experienced as pleasant. If the transformation is not successful there are two possibilities. The dream may be experienced as an unpleasant one (a nightmare) because a forbidden wish is gratified. Alternatively the dreamer may waken before the dream is completed, so that the forbidden wish remains unsatisfied.

Dreams are fascinating things, and experienced therapists make considerable use of them. The novice is advised to be sparing of dream analysis. This is not to say that he must never discuss them, but he should be wary if his patient produces nothing but dreams for discussion. When this happens the patient may be avoiding the examination of other psychological material.

Symbolism

There is often much repetition in the patient's story and in his account of his doings. Different events may reveal an underlying similarity, being repeated with different characters. Other happenings may repeated with different characters. Other happenings may repeat themselves in allegorical form.

A large part of the therapist's task is to identify themes which are repeated; comparing them with each other; defining an underlying pattern and ultimately deducing their origins. Symbols are often used extensively. An instance of this has already been given in the example in which a patient dreamt that he was shaking hands with his friend. Here, the hand symbolised the male genitalia, and the handshake symbolised mutual masturbation. The word 'masturbates' was imposed on the dream in the form of a name, 'Master Bates', which was recognised by the dreamer as 'wrong'—in retrospect, in more than one way.

Preoccupation with *recent* events often results from their value as symbolic reproductions of earlier experiences. Certain people may form a symbolic whole. Thus people in authority such as the Sovereign, teachers, political leaders, employers, policemen, and so on, form a group. Ultimately they may represent the parents. Activities which are rhythmic and repetitive may be symbols for sexual activity, whilst such activities as losing, or forgetting things, or departing on a journey, may symbolise hostility to, and a wish to eradicate the people with whom the things or ideas are associated.

Many events which originate in early life when they are but dimly comprehended or perhaps are completely misunderstood, may be repeated in symbolic form in later life. They may appear to have a sinister significance. This is quickly repressed, but it may break through *repeatedly* in allegorical form—perhaps as a neurotic symptom. If the original event was established before the development of logical thought, it will not be understood in terms of adult logic. The therapist must be willing to abandon his own sense of *logical* understanding in such cases, so that he may comprehend the patient's *non-logical* productions.

Interlude on Non-Logic

PROOF: That the reader will ride the next winner of the Grand National.

LET	$x=y$
then	$xy=y^2$
and	$x^2-xy=x^2-y^2$
Factorize	$x(x-y)=(x+y)(x-y)$
Divide both sides by $(x-y)$	$x=x+y$
BUT $x=y$ so	$x=2x$
Divide both sides by x	$1=2$

SINCE the reader and the person who will ride the next winner of the Grand National are two

AND $\qquad 1=2$

THEN the reader and the person who will ride the next winner of the Grand National are one.

THEREFORE the reader will ride the next winner of the Grand National. Q.E.D.

There must be a catch in it somewhere (there is). If not, it is magic, for how else can someone be changed into the winner of the most famous horse race in the world? Patients frequently seek magic from their therapist. Sometimes they protest that they know he cannot achieve the impossible: that they do not hope for miracles: that they know that their therapist is only human. Nevertheless, often there is a strong feeling that the therapist ought to be a fairy godmother, and that *surely*, there is someone in the world who is. The most frequent complaint about psychotherapists is that they are unable to turn dross into gold. Since non-logicality plays so large a part in the development of problems they encounter and in the hopes that patients have for their solution, we must spend some time in examining the significance of magic and non-logic.

The very young child believes in magic. This is encouraged in most families. He is told that at Christmas time, if he is very good, Father Christmas will come down the chimney (even if none exists) and fill his stocking with the toys he wants. Young children know about fairyland and many have funny uncles who can perform magical tricks. They make money appear from thin air. The child does not look for the trick in all this, because for him there is no trick. Magic exists.

The problem about magic is that there can be bad magic as well as good. Good magic is all very well, but bad magic is very frightening. It is equated with blackness and darkness, and the child trembles with fear when the house is dark and all is quiet.

The stories which entrance children are about fairies and witches, magicians and hobgoblins, whose judicious interaction leads to the rescue of the hero from a hopeless predicament. In these stories, the race is never to the swift, but to people like the child himself: the small and feeble: the seventh son of a seventh son, or the youngest of three brothers. Maturity and experience are equated with ugliness and wickedness. The young and beautiful live happily ever after: the old are subjected to punishments which are particularly vile and bloody. Their feet are chopped off, they are thrown to the wolves, or they are dropped into boiling oil.

The author is not making a value judgement about this. He is not saying that we should deny the existence of magic to our children; or that in some way the idea is harmful. The child *believes* in magic and that is a fact.

Adults believe in magic, too. As this is being written, the newspapers are full of stories of a man who can cause spoons to bend by occult means. Thousands believe that such a thing is possible and hundreds try to emulate him. It is a pretty harmless piece of magic (if it is magic) but a rather pointless one. Unfortunately, it does not seem possible to reverse the process.

There are other things, not so easily recognised as magic, but magic nevertheless. There is the magic of the advertiser. People really believe that they can learn to speak a foreign language in 24 hours, to play the piano in six weeks or to lose weight without eating less. They believe that a seven stone weakling can be changed into a muscle man. Although we may not be very sure about an after-life, we have our children baptised to be on the safe side. There is the magic of gambling and of the football pools (the adult equivalent of turning dross into gold). Hire purchase enables the individual to find that crock of gold which allows him to purchase the car for which he yearns. It may be that he will repent at leisure, but that is irrelevant, since there may be other magic around the corner. We are assured, and we believe, that all our troubles will disappear if we adopt the principles of one or other political party, or if we rid ourselves of the trade union leaders, the bosses, or of ethnic groups which are different from our own.

Adults enjoy their fairy tales, too. The heroes of adult fiction are rescued by astonishing coincidences which, if they really occurred, would certainly be ascribed to divine intervention.

But if there is only one *real* magician in the world, all the striving, struggling, competing; all the difficulty and distress of life can be overcome. There will be no need of psychotherapists or counsellors, no need of doctors, no need for suffering, no need for working. Indeed, the idea of magic is a very attractive one.

It is much easier to demonstrate to people that magic exists than to convince them that it does not. We all hold on, with extraordinary tenacity, to belief in telepathy, extrasensory perception and other 'paranormal' phenomena. We believe in lucky charms, good omens, black practices. Almost no-one is able to walk under a ladder without any concern whatsoever. Some people acknowledge the superstition 'in case there is something in it'. Others cross the road well in advance, so that the secret of their superstition is protected. Some walk around the ladder because 'it is the sensible thing to do...someone may be up it'. Some, to show that they are *not* superstitious, walk defiantly under it, perhaps crossing their fingers as they do so, and heaving a sigh of relief when the ordeal is over. Very few really do not care.

Magic overpowers logic. Much of human thinking accepts magic and so ignores logic. In psychotherapy, however, there is no magic. The therapist may tolerate his patient's belief in it, because by doing so he can help him search it out and examine its origins, applying the necessary corrections of reality. People may be ashamed of their belief in the non-logical and are often reluctant to discuss it. Yet, unless it is discussed, its true non-logicality can neither be exposed, examined nor corrected. Just as dividing both sides of an equation by $(x-y)$ strikes at the root of mathematical magic in the case where $x=y$, (for you may not divide both sides by zero) and thereby allows the reader to win a horse race, so one tiny non-logical assumption can turn a mouse into a man or a pauper into a prince.

Personal logic often has an internal consistency, although it is obviously non-logical to the outside world. In order to comprehend his patient's difficulties it may be necessary for the therapist to understand this logic. An example is given by the case of a patient who had been married twice. Speaking of her *previous* marriage she said, 'When my second husband was alive...' Quickly she realised that she had made a slip of the tongue (the reader will note that it has a double implication) and corrected herself. The therapist asked 'Who was your first husband?' There was a thoughful pause. Then she said 'There was a boy I idolised. I was only 13 at the time. He took me out once or twice. He wasn't very interested in me. Then I saw him out with someone else...' At this point, she burst into tears and said 'I can still remember how it hurt. Funny...I had forgotten all about it.' Her problem centred on the relationship with her present husband, and his death would have been one solution to her difficulties. This was the second meaning of her slip. When a psychological phenomenon is caused by more than one factor, as in this case, the phenomenon is said to be an example of over-, or multiple-determination.

Non-logicality arises frequently in respect of emotions, and a few everyday example will be given. One of the most common non-logical fears is that of small animals. Strong men may blench at the sight of a spider, and a graphic description of such a man struggling with a spider in the bath is given by Michael Flanders:

> I have faced a charging bull in Barcelona,
> I have dragged a mountain lioness from her cub,
> I've restored a mad gorilla to its owner,
> But I don't dare face that spider in the tub.
> What a frightful looking beast,
> Half an inch across at least,
> It would frighten even Superman or Garth;
> There's contempt it can't disguise,
> In the little beady eyes
> Of the spider sitting glowering in the bath.

Women may scream at the sight of a mouse; mothers may squirm when their little ones bring them a big, fat, juicy worm from the garden. There is nothing logical in all this. Obviously it is the small animal which should really be afraid. Illogical fears such as these are almost universal.

Specific fears which are illogical are called *phobias*. Common examples include fears of height, and fears of being alone. Pathological varieties include fear of domestic animals (especially of cats), of going out of the house, and of being in crowds. Patients with phobias such as these experience fear, and although the fear may not be logical, nevertheless it is fear.

Phobias may have a magical quality. What can it be that leads to a fear of leaving the house, of being shut in a room or of finding oneself in a crowd of people? The patient will say that he does not know, and of course, he does not. It is illogical. How does it happen that a patient may be plagued with horrible thoughts concerning the death of someone whom he loves dearly? It is not logical. The therapist must be prepared to tolerate non-logic, and to be willing to look at the implications so that he can help the patient understand them.

Some emotions appear to be illogical because they refer to an event which is remote in time. Time is supposed to cure everything. But time is a *logical* concept, and the non-logical takes no note of it. Emotions which were aroused many years previously may continue to operate long after the events which precipitated them have been forgotten. The most striking example occurs when a mourning process lies fallow for many years. If the circumstances of the death can be 'relived' the patient may also relive the associated emotion, and weep bitterly. He may say that he feels ashamed at his distress about something that happened so long ago. Nevertheless the emotion is there, and it is best to be expressed. Other emotions may be recalled likewise: for example the memory of a situation which appeared terrifying at the time ('little things' may seem very frightening to children) or the anger at some indignity that had long been forgotten. The expression of such half-forgotten emotions is called *catharsis*.

One final group of non-logical emotions refers to sensitivities. These are of particular importance to young people and the therapist must be wary of dismissing them as trivial or irrelevant. A small spot of acne may feel to a sensitive adolescent like a flaming beacon, and he should not be discouraged from saying so. Older people have sensitivities too: perhaps about a bodily feature like the size or shape of the nose, or the colour of the hair. Some patients have a sense of 'intellectual' inferiority: they may be ignorant of a subject with which they feel they should be familiar.

The therapist is often tempted to 'reassure' about sensitivities, and to indicate that they do not really matter. But if they exist, they matter to the patient, and 'reassurance' is more likely to confirm the patient's belief that they are truly something about which to be concerned.

Non-logicality may present itself in unwanted thoughts. The patient may be plagued with the idea that someone he loves dearly is dead, or is about to die, or perhaps is seriously injured. He will protest that these thoughts are horrible, yet he is unable to free himself of them. He may be oppressed with ideas of harming people whom he loves, or of indulging in a sickening sexual perversion. He says 'I do not wish to think about such things. I know I would not *do* them: I know I *could* not do them. Yet the ideas keep coming. It is horrible.'

The management of the non-logical follows the same pattern as that described for other psychological conditions. The therapist attends, listens, and endeavours to understand. He never condemns, 'explains', or tries to reassure. He examines the material for its possible outcome. He pays particular attention to the consequences which would follow if the unwanted idea were to be fulfilled. What would it be like for a housewife who is confined to her house with a travel phobia, if she were to be released from her bond? The usual response is 'Oh, it would be wonderful'. But the therapist must ask 'Would it really be wonderful?' There would be advantages of course, but there may be disadvantages, too. What are the *disadvantages* of being freed from a phobia?

People who have obsessional thoughts about death, destruction or degrading perversions should be encouraged to imagine what it would be like if the dread thing were to happen. Of course, it would be horrible, but would there be something positive to balance the horror? Could there even be an advantage? Phobias about specific objects or centred on specific situations will usually require an examination of the symbolic meaning of the situation or object.

Gain

The advantages of being psychopathic or neurotic*. The psychopath is allowed to talk to himself, which is very handy when he wants the railway carriage to himself.

The neurotic is not obliged to fetch the coal in as when his wife requests him to do so all he need do is throw down his paper and scream: 'Coal, coal, coal! Does nobody think about anything else but coal?'

The psychopath is not required to shave, thereby not having to indulge in backchat with barbers about the prospects for Sheffield Wednesday.

The neurotic need not keep abreast of world affairs since his only observation of these need be: 'Politics, politics, politics—they make me vomit.'

The psychopath does not have to take a bath and is, therefore, less prone to catching cold, grippe, influenza or bath rash.

The neurotic always gets prompt attention from tradesmen who are terrified of him.

The psychopath may play yo-yo in public.

The neurotic always has right of way on the roads.

The psychopath is not expected to have a job, thereby not running the risk, which would otherwise be acute, of getting the sack.

It may seem strange to think that something as disagreeable as illness might have advantages, but reflection will confirm that there is something to be gained, even from the most serious of diseases. For example, a patient with advanced cancer will be relieved of the anxieties and the burdens which might be his lot if he were healthy. It is not asserted that anyone would wish to be ill. But illness brings a few comforts, although they might be cheerfully surrendered in favour of good health. The advantages of an illness, whether physical or psychological, are called its secondary gain, and they must always be taken into account in treatment. A patient with a serious but not fatal illness (for example, a per-

*Selected from *Maybe you're Just Inferior* by Herald Froy.

forated peptic ulcer) may make extraordinarily rapid progress at first. Then, unaccountably, his rate of progress slows as he becomes stronger. He develops new evanescent symptoms which require further investigation. The results may be ambiguous. The therapist begins to have a vague suspicion that for some reason thepatient does not really *want* to get well. When his social situation is explored, the suspicion may become a near certainty. Perhaps the patient is a housewife with an aggressive, undemonstrative, husband; a growing, demanding, family, and with little time for relaxation. In hospital she is visited regularly, treated with concern and sympathy, deferred to, and given every consideration. It would be almost *abnormal* for her to wish to return home. The secondary gain of the illness has become paramount.

Psychoneurotic illness usually provides *primary* gain. By the nature of her illness the housebound housewife obtains many of the benefits of a patient in hospital. These represent the secondary gain. Her *primary* gain is to set aside a conflict in which the opposing factors may be almost evenly balanced. Sometimes she feels herself unloved and unwanted, and her reaction might be to leave her neglectful husband. On the other hand she wishes to stay with him, for like Mrs Burton she *loves* him. The development of a psychological illness, characterised by a fear of leaving the house, solves the conflict. She is no longer able to leave her husband even if she would. The primary gain of the illness is that the problem is resolved.

Ambivalence

Most people are aware of variations in their attitudes towards people who are important to them. They may at one time love them dearly: at other times they find them infuriating. This fluctuation in feeling is part of every day experience. The word 'ambivalence' is used for the *simultaneous* experience of opposing feelings. Ambivalence is partly unconscious and it is non-logical. The individual is *consciously* aware only of the predominant attitude. In the case of Mrs Burton (Chapter I) she loved her husband but simultaneously she hated him for not behaving as she would wish. Consciously, she was unaware of her dislike. It could have shown itself in unconscious activities. She might, for example, have 'accidentally' sugared his tea with salt, or she might have a dream—she would call it a nightmare—that he was dead.

The word 'ambivalence' is used in a different and rather restricted sense to describe certain aspects of alternating *behaviour* in patients suffering from schizophrenia. The therapist may offer to shake hands with the patient but he receives no response. So he withdraws his hand, and as he does so the patient presents his. The therapist moves his hand towards the patient again but now the patient withdraws his. So it goes on. The reader should be clear of this meaning of the word 'ambivalence' when it is used in this context.

Free association

Free association is a fundamental technique of psychoanalysis (q.v.). The patient allows his thoughts to run free without any *conscious* attempt to direct, select or modify them. One thought leads to another, then to the next and so on. The patient is asked to report whatever comes into his mind, whether or not it appears to be relevant, important, offensive, embarrassing, disloyal or anything else; and irrespective of whether it seems in any way related to what has gone before. During therapy the unconscious threads are unravelled and analysed.

A classical example of free association and the way in which it proceeds is given by Freud.

Freud was travelling with a young man who was familiar with some of his publications. During the course of their conversation the young man wished to recall a quotation from Virgil. However, one word—*aliquis*—although on the tip of his tongue, refused to come to him, and to conceal the gap, he changed the order of the words of the quotation. He knew that the order was wrong, and he knew that Freud knew that it was wrong! In his exasperation, he exclaimed 'Please don't look so scornful. There's something missing in the line; how does the whole thing really go?'

Probably smiling, Freud gave the correct quotation. The young man answered "How stupid to forget a word like aliquis!" Then he thought for a moment and added "You claim that one never forgets a thing without some reason. I should be very curious to learn how I came to forget the word *aliquis* in this case". Freud answered, "That should not take us long. I must only ask you tell me, *candidly* and *uncritically*, whatever comes into your mind if you direct your attention to the forgotten word without any definite aim".

The young man answered 'There springs to my mind the ridiculous notion of dividing the word up like this: *a* and *liquis*.' There was a pause and Freud said 'What occurs to you next?' Slowly his companion replied *'Relics, liquifying, fluidity, fluid'*. Freud told him to continue and he said 'I am thinking of *Simon of Trent* whose relics I saw two years ago... My next thoughts are about an article that I read lately in an Italian newspaper. Its title, I think, was "What St *Augustine* says about Women". What do you make of that?' Freud merely answered, 'I am waiting'. And the young man went on 'I am thinking of a fine old gentleman I met last week. His name was *Benedict*.'

At this point Freud drew together some of the threads he had perceived. 'Here are a row of Saints: St *Simon*, St *Augustine*, St *Benedict*'. This intervention had the effect of bringing to his companion's mind another thought. He continued 'Now it is St *Januarius* and the miracle of his blood that comes into my mind' and he added something which is charactistic of free association: '...my thoughts seem to me to be running on mechanically'. Freud commented that St *Januarius* and

St *Augustine* both have to do with the calendar. 'But won't you remind me about the miracle of his blood?' he asked. The young man answered 'Surely you must have heard of that? They keep the blood of St Januarius in a phial inside a church at *Naples,* and on a particular holy day it miraculously *liquifies.* The people attach great importance to this miracle and get very excited if it's delayed, as happened once at a time when the French were occupying the town. So the General in command took the reverend gentleman aside and gave him to understand, with an unmistakeable gesture towards the soldiers posted outside, that he *hoped* the miracle would take place very soon. And in fact it did take place...'

At this point the young man paused, and Freud asked 'Well, go on. Why do you pause?' 'Well', he replied 'something *has* come into my mind...but it's too intimate to pass on...besides, I don't see any connection...' Readers who are not familiar with this episode might wish to speculate what the 'something' might be.

Freud replied 'Then you mustn't insist on learning from me how you came to forget your *aliquis.*' Thereupon the young man continued 'Well then I've suddenly thought of a lady from whom I might easily hear a piece of news that would be very awkward for both of us'. Freud said, 'That her periods have stopped?' Astonished, his companion asked, 'How could you guess that?' Freud answered 'Think of the *calendar saints, the blood that starts to flow on a particular day, the disturbance when the event fails to take place, the open threats* that the miracle must be vouchsafed or else...In fact you've made use of the miracle of St Januarius to manufacture a brilliant allusion to women's periods'. The young man asked whether it was this 'anxious expectation that made me unable to produce an unimportant word like *aliquis'*?

Freud answered 'It seems to me undeniable: You need only recall the division you made into *a-liquis* and your associations: *relics, liquifying, fluid.* St Simon was *sacrificed as a child'* (as though he had been aborted). The young man confessed that the lady concerned was an Italian with whom he had been to Naples.

This example of the forgetting of a word which had a significant unconscious connection occurred in a healthy man, not a neurotic patient. Admittedly he is likely to have been worried. We may wonder why he challenged Freud to explain his lapse. Perhaps it was with the knowledge that Freud was a doctor, and in the hope that Freud would tell him how an abortion might be procured.

In a footnote, Freud mentions that when his companion was searching for the missing word, the word 'exoriare' had thrust itself upon him with 'peculiar clarity and obstinacy'. His association with 'exoriare' was *exorcism.* Freud comments that exorcism might be a symbolic substitute for getting rid of the unwanted child by abortion.

The transference

Patients have feelings about their doctors. Usually they like them. A patient who dislikes his doctor will, if he can, change to someone else. The feelings may be quite unrealistic. Some patients think of their doctors with a degree of awe and admiration which may seem quite absurd to the objective observer. The most drunken and incompetent doctor may be praised for his skill and knowledge, and the smell on his breath dismissed as a charming eccentricity.

The feeling which a patient has for his therapist is called the transference. Since the patient knows very little about his therapist, and since by the principle of anonymity (see Chapter 6) the therapist maintains his patient's ignorance about him to a maximum, it is necessary to consider the nature of these feelings, whence they come, and what they signify.

Transference feelings may be positive or negative and of any degree of strength. Very strong positive feelings are akin to love. The patient is constantly preoccupied with thoughts of his therapist, and longs to be with him all the time. He tries to discover everything about him, and to do all that he can to please him. He may wander the streets in the hope of catching a glimpse of him. The emergence of a strong positive transference is the origin of the common belief that patients fall in love with their psychotherapists. When the patient experiences a transference such as this, the original problem is no longer of importance, except as a means of holding on to his therapist. His primary concern is how he may express his overwhelming affection for his therapist. A strong positive transference is of no value in helping the patient to overcome his problem—indeed, it may have precisely the opposite effect.

A strong negative transference is similar to hate. Again, the patient is constantly preoccupied with thoughts about his therapist. He wishes to subdue him, to demonstrate his weakness and fallibility, to conquer him, to destroy him. Subjugation is now infinitely more important than solving a problem, and a strong negative transference will remove any possibility of a solution. The patient would never allow his foe to have the satisfaction of knowing that he had in any way assisted with a cure.

A moderate positive transference is of help in therapy. The patient likes his therapist, is grateful for the efforts which are made for him, wishes to co-operate, but does not mind risking the therapist's occasional displeasure by disagreeing with him, or even defying him. A moderate negative transference hinders therapy. It is manifested by a falling-off of interest, the postponement of consultations for trivial or inadequate reasons, and perhaps eventually cessation of therapy.

Transference reactions vary in the same patient from time to time. A strong positive transference may give way to a strong negative one. Elements of both positive and negative transference can often be discerned simultaneously.

Detection of transference

The patient may use various devices in order to defeat the principle of anonymity. He may refer to books which the therapist might have read (but usually has not), or use colloquial foreign phrases with which the therapist should be familiar (but usually is not). By these means, the patient is endeavouring to gauge the direction of the therapist's interests.

It is wise not to embark upon an intellectual exchange on these occasions. If the therapist is acquainted with the work in question, or understands the meaning of the phrase which is used, he may be assured that the patient will refer to other books, or use other phrases with which he is not familiar. He should always request the patient to explain his allusion, always to use English and so on.

At other times the patient will indicate his feelings in a piecemeal way, often through 'innocent' non-sequiturs, in the course of which he tries to find out about the therapist's opinions, his prejudices, his interests and his attitudes. Here are some examples:

He may say 'I do like that tie'. The therapist may question, 'and the person who is wearing it?'

The patient may ask 'Isn't Wilson/Heath an awful man?' Here he plays his hunch and appeals to what he presumes to be the political prejudices of the therapist.

He may say 'Don't you get tired of listening to people's problems all day long?' and the therapist will wonder if he is asking 'Do you get tired of me?'

One patient said 'Dr O used to recommend Friar's Balsam. He was a *very* clever doctor' and the therapist wondered, 'Don't you wish you had him instead of me?'

The patient may put the question, 'What sort of person are you?' by asking 'What do you do at the weekends?' He may ask if the therapist is 'available' by enquiring whether he is married, if the therapist has a sex life by asking if he has children. He may wonder whether his therapist ever gets angry with him, but ask instead, 'Do you get angry with your children?'

Where does the transference come from?

In an attempt to answer this question, we must return to the patient's original expectation of his therapist: that he is omniscient and omnipotent, powerful, worldly-wise, and able to offer a helping hand to the poor creatures who come to him for assistance.

The therapist does not contradict this view. Instead he tries to help the patient put it into words. He also makes it clear to the patient that he wishes him to tell whatever he thinks, wishes and feels. The things which are 'confessed' may seem very trivial to the therapist, although they may occasionally be matters of great magnitude. The therapist never criticises or condemns his patient for these confessions. Acceptance may be a form of love to the patient, and he may come to love his therapist in turn. On the other hand, the therapist is unable to tell the patient what he should do. The patient may then feel that his therapist is denying him something to which he is entitled, in return for what has been told. Such deprivation may ultimately lead him to hate his therapist. When he expresses his hate, he is on the alert for the therapist's response. The therapist has said that he can— indeed that he must—put his feelings into words. What will the therapist feel, when this is done? Will he really remain non-judgemental?

For his part, the therapist endeavours to stick to the terms of the contract, to accept whatever is said, without condemnation. The patient again feels grateful for this, and the negative transference begins to dissolve.

Expression of the transference, whether it is negative or positive, is the first step towards its resolution. Verbalisation precedes resolution. When the transference has reached manageable proportions, the constructive work of psychotherapy can continue.

The seeds of the transference reaction are likely to have been sown in the remote past, when the patient experienced similar feelings towards another person whose relationship with him was similar to that of therapist. That person was imagined to be all-knowing and all-powerful. Probably he was a parent: sometimes another relative or a teacher. When the storm of powerful transference feelings has passed, the patient may recall that once, long ago, he felt like that towards someone else. It may be possible to detect the transference reaction in the patient's attitude towards similar figures throughout his life. He can be forewarned that a similar thing may happen in the future, if the circumstances repeat themselves.

Resolution of the transference

The transference should be interpreted whenever it is discerned. Examples have already been given. Discussion, dissection, analysis and verbalisation will lead to its resolution and often to its latent origins. It is sometimes appropriate to ask the patient, 'What can it be that is so attractive about someone of whom you know so little?' The transference may be interpreted in terms of the 'here and now' situation. How does the patient react to the therapist at this *very moment*. What significance has his behaviour?

The counter transference

The therapist, of course, has feelings for his patient, and these too may be positive or negative. If they are negative from the outset, the therapist will usually find a rational excuse for avoiding any formal therapy ('He would not be amenable to the type of treatment which is employed here.') Therapy is offered usually to patients for whom the therapist has a moderate positive counter-transference. As time passes, the therapist may find himself developing fluctuating counter-transferences and he should be prepared to examine the reasons for these, in his own personality.

The therapist's feelings about the transference of his patient may itself be an indication of his counter-transference. He may feel hurt and offended if the patient becomes hostile towards him. Perhaps he feels that he has tried his best, yet he receives no gratitude. It is not pleasant to be condemned by a patient, even less so if the condemnation seems to have some foundation in fact.

Interpretation of a patient's positive transference ('It seems as though you are very fond of me') may be embarrassing for the therapist, particularly when his own feelings towards the patient are neutral, and more so when they are more positive.

It is not uncommon, especially in physical medicine, for a doctor to assure a patient that he knows 'exactly what it feels like, because I have had the same thing myself' going on then to share his experience. This custom is not necessarily of any value to the patient. Toothache is not alleviated if the patient knows that his doctor also has toothache. Usually, the doctor is unlikely to recall the *actual* experience, because he will have taken rapid steps to alleviate it. Sharing of experience is of little value to the patient, and conflicts with the principle of anonymity. The therapist is advised not to engage in it.

Management of the counter-transference. The therapist should not tell the patient about his counter-transference. If he wishes, he will usually be able to discover its origins for himself. If he feels that it could get out of hand—if, for example, the therapist finds himself falling in love with his patient, he *must* seek the assistance of a trusted and experienced colleague. There are unfortunate occasions on which a therapist permits the relationship to continue beyond the limits of what is ethically acceptable as a result of his positive counter-transference. If this should happen the therapist *must* seek the assistance of a colleague. The task of the colleague is to help the therapist deal with his counter-transference, not to bring professional disgrace upon him. In such circumstances as these it is usually necessary for the therapist to stop treating the patient, who may complain that he has been sacrificed. It is not easy to refute such a complaint. A new therapist may offer to take the case, but the patient will feel very ill-used.

6.   The Mechanical Details

CARDINAL PRINCIPLE: The rule of anonymity.

It is desirable that the background of psychotherapy should be organised carefully, so that everything proceeds as expeditiously as possible. In this chapter we will examine some aspects of the procedure which are often taken for granted. In doing so it is necessary to bear in mind two points. The first is that the patient's natural curiosity about his therapist should be encouraged to follow its own fantasies as freely as.possible. This means that the therapist must remain as anonymous as possible, so that his patient's imagination is not impeded by an excess of reality. Everything that the therapist does and says may have a meaning for the patient, just as everything that the patient does and says has a meaning for the therapist.

The second point is that, since therapy is the principal task of the therapist, he should free himself as far as possible from work that can be done effectively by others. When things run smoothly, free of unnecessary distractions, the patient is given ideal circumstances to perform his part of therapy and to make the best use of the opportunities which are offered to him.

The location

Psychotherapy could be practised in the home of either the therapist or the patient, 'somewhere else', or in an office or consulting room. These alternatives will now be considered.

The therapist's home

Patients are naturally curious about what sort of life the therapist leads, and may sometimes 'just happen' to pass the house in which he lives. If he is to practise from his own home, much of the purpose of the rule of anonymity will be defeated. Many things which are personal to the therapist will be apparent to the patient, and whilst his curiosity will be satisfied, he will lose the opportunity of developing fantasies about his therapist. Therapists and counsellors are advised against practising from their own homes.

It may occasionally happen that a patient will call at the therapist's home, asking to discuss a matter of great urgency which has just arisen. This may well be his wish, but the patient should be told that he must make an appointment, and that it is not possible for him to be seen in any other way.

Incidentally for his own sake, it is desirable that the therapist should have a place in which he can feel free to relax in his own way, free from the demands of his work and his patients. His own home is the appropriate place for this purpose.

The patient's home

If his own home is chosen, the patient will often make special preparation for the therapist's visit, especially in the early stages, whilst the therapist may find that he has to compete with an apparently unending series of telephone calls, curious children, barking dogs, door-to-door salesmen and visits from the neighbours. For the therapist is the patient's guest, and, in a sense, he must defer to his host. If the patient should be alone in the house, and if he and the therapist are of opposite sexes, the therapist may find himself in a rather compromising situation, both from the point of view of the patient and also from that of inquisitive neighbours. Furthermore the patient may lose the opportunity of 'acting out' some of his transference feelings. He cannot so easily 'forget' to attend for his appointment, and although he may storm out of the counselling room, it is not nearly so convenient to storm out of his own house, leaving the therapist in possession. The patient will not have the benefit of a slow, reflective journey back to his own home after the session: something which may be of particular importance if its content has been distressing for him. Instead he must immediately resume his place in the household.

On the whole, therefore, it is best not to undertake intensive psychotherapy in the patient's own home. There may be occasions nevertheless when this is forced upon the therapist—or more often upon the counsellor—for example, when the client is house-bound, perhaps on account of some physical handicap, or when the agency for which the counsellor works requires that the client be visited at home. However the counsellor should understand that arrangements such as these are second best.

'Somewhere'

Once in a while, the patient may suggest that he meets the therapist not in his office, or in his home, but 'somewhere else'. The significance of such a proposal is obvious, and must be interpreted. It is an endeavour to change the relationship from a professional one to a social (and probably intimate) one. It should never be accepted. The therapist should not consent to any clandestine arrangment which might place him in a position which he could have cause to regret subsequently.

The office or consulting room

This, without any question, is the most suitable location for psychotherapy. Usually it is 'neutral' territory, often chosen and furnished by someone else. It is impersonal (although not necessarily unwelcoming) and thereby protects the therapist's anonymity. Usually there are people about if the therapist should find himself in an unexpected difficulty. The patient can stay away if he does not like what is happening, or if he has kept his appointment, he may walk out.

When, as a result of such circumstances as have already been mentioned, the counsellor is forced to visit the client in his own home, the meeting place should be transfered as soon as possible to the counsellor's office. The office is the therapist's work room. It is provided for the specific purpose of psychotherapy, not for relaxation, and helps the patient understand that psychotherapy is work, not just some sort of social interchange.

The ideal consulting room is smaller than a ballroom and larger than a telephone kiosk. Since it is usually provided by someone else, its size may not be ideal. If the therapist has a choice, he should choose the room in which *he* feels most comfortable. It is to be *his* work room, and if he finds it uncomfortable he can hardly expect the patient to feel easy.

The room should be well lit, and as quiet as possible. There should be provision for switching incoming telephone calls to the secretary, so that quietness may be preserved. When there is only one window, the therapist must sit in the shade, and the patient must sit facing the light. Patients often complain that the therapist can see them, but that they cannot see him. This is an expression of the patient's wish to know more about his therapist and of his fear that the therapist may know too much about him. Realistically, it is much more important that the therapist should see the patient, than that the patient should see the therapist.

Furniture

The chairs should be comfortable and reasonably firm. The therapist spends much time in his chair, and he should have the more comfortable one. The *position* of the chairs is important. The patient's is placed so that he is well lit. The therapist's chair should be placed at right angles with it, fairly close, but not so close that he and the patient kick one another if they change the position of their legs. The therapist should not sit directly opposite the patient (for otherwise he would *always* be within his patient's field of vision) neither should the two sit side by side. The right angled position enables the therapist to pay close attention to the patient. If the patient looks straight ahead he sees only the room. He needs to turn his head slightly in order to see the therapist.

When there is a desk, it should not be used to separate the therapist from his patient. It may be placed out of the way, in another part of the room. Some doctors use a desk to separate themselves physically from their patients. This is not desirable in psychotherapy. The desk itself should be uncluttered. It is not designed to demonstrate to the world what a busy person the therapist is, or how untidy he is.

The style of decoration and the pictures which hang in the room are the responsibility of the people who provide it. Personal photographs conflict with the principle of anonymity and they should not be used.

An ample supply of paper handkerchiefs, an ashtray and a carafe of water should be available. If he wishes to take notes during the session the therapist may use a clip-board to support them. Some people use a tape-recorder, but there is seldom enough time to play back the recording, so that a recorder rapidly loses its novelty value. When one is used, the patient is likely to have fantasies about the use to which the tape is put ('...what sort of people listen to the recordings...?') It is probably better not to use one.

The Couch

The couch is a focus of fictional psychiatry but its regular use in psychotherapy occurs only in psychoanalysis (q.v.). The patient lies supine, in a good light and the analyst sits at the head of the couch and to one side. He can see the patient but the patient is unable to see him.

This has a number of implications. The patient, unable to see the therapist, can only imagine his responses. He may wonder whether the analyst is smiling or laughing at him, or whether he is asleep. The therapist is truly a tabula rasa and the transference is built on even less reality than when patient and therapist face one another. In his supine position the patient may feel exceedingly passive. Sometimes he may feel like a child who has been sent to bed. The couch may be a place of romance, and the patient's erotic fantasies may be stimulated.

When they come first for psychotherapy, patients often expect to be told to lie on a couch and some are rather disappointed when this does not happen. Psychotherapists other than psychoanalysts do not necessarily make use of the couch, but those who do should explore with the patient what he feels about lying on it. Novices sometimes use a couch in order to impress their patients with the profundity of their calling. They would be wise to examine their own motives first, especially if the patient is blonde and female, and they are male and hungry.

The Therapist

It has been emphasised already that the patient will read a great deal into small hints, and that he will try to discover all that he can about his therapist. The therapist should dress in a way appropriate to his calling. 'Way out' dress is not really suitable, especially when one is dealing with sick people.

Most junior medical students and some doctors wear stethoscopes round their necks, in the same way that cannibals wear beads of

human teeth and brothel-keepers place red lamps outside their pre-
mises: to proclaim their trade without ambiguity. Some therapists
wear a white coat as their badge of office. Some therapists refuse to
wear white coats, because they do not wish to be identified with those
who do. Others consider that white coats present a barrier to the
patient. The whole subject is very complicated. The author does not
wear a white coat. If he has been using one, he sometimes leaves his
stethoscope on his desk. He has given up trying to understand why.
He is proud of his job, makes sure that his patients know what it is,
and is aware of no particular need either to advertise it or to conceal it.

The therapist must act with courtesy towards the patient at all times.
He should not indulge himself in the luxury of losing his temper with
his patient. There are apocryphal stories of the beneficial outcome
which has resulted when the great have told their patients exactly
what they thought of them. The novice is advised to avoid such
dubious precepts.

The therapist expects his patient to exert considerable self-discipline
and he himself should provide an example whenever possible. The
sessions should start and finish on time. If there is much to be said,
and time is running out, the patient can be told that the story will
be continued at the next session. If the therapist expects to be delayed,
he should try to arrange for a message to be passed through, and when
the time comes a proper apology should be offered. No explanation
should be offered however tempting it may be. ('. . . His Royal High-
ness was having another bad turn . . .') If the session is to be a short
one, the patient should be warned of this at the outset.

It has been indicated that the therapist offers the patient his close,
uncritical, attention. By 'uncritical' is meant not only that the therapist
should not condemn his patient, but that neither should he praise
him. If the therapist praises on some occasions, 'non-praise' becomes
equivalent to condemnation. It is best to avoid evaluation completely.

The therapist and patient do not normally touch one another.
Some therapists shake hands with their patients at the beginning of
a session and when they part. There is no objection to this, provided
that it is done routinely, with all patients, and on the understanding
that it is the reflection of a social convention. The handshake should
never be prolonged, either as a sign of encouragement, or praise, or
for any other reason.

Ancillary personnel

A competent receptionist is invaluable. She takes much of the
administrative work off his shoulders, so that the therapist is able to
give his whole attention to the patient. She keeps the diary, makes
the appointments, answers the telephone and welcomes patients. She
takes messages, looks after children and animals, and makes the tea.

The patient will often chat with her informally, sometimes revealing important information, in the hope that in her turn, the receptionist will pass it on to the therapist. However She is too wise to be caught in this way. She says 'You must tell that to the doctor yourself'. She is firm, sensible, trustworthy and reliable and, in her own way, quite as important as the therapist. One would expect such paragons to be very few and far between: the author has perhaps been unusually fortunate, for he has known many.

The job of receptionist is usually combined with that of the secretary. She is responsible for correspondence, looks after the notes and sends follow-up letters to patients who default.

There may be other people to whom the therapist can turn for advice: lawyers, clergymen, social workers, and other therapists. He may seek a second opinion from them (see page 84), but unless they are to take the case over they are his assistants, not his masters.

Procedure

It is the practice of the author to adhere fairly strictly to the ethical rule, that specialists should accept patients only from other doctors. He does not, therefore, accept self-referrals. He expects that the consultation will have the knowledge and approval of the family doctor. In his experience any attempt to bypass this rule often leads to difficulty and inconvenience and sometimes to embarrassment. In the long run, the patient always suffers. The patient who is unable to trust his family doctor should be advised to find one whom he can trust. Therapists who work in the paramedical professions will usually accept patients only if they are referred by a doctor. Members of the voluntary counselling organisations usually accept self-referrals.

In general, it is desirable that the patient should be seen by appointment, for which he should write or telephone. The therapist will be assisted if he has some information about the patient's background from the person who has made the referral. *The first interview* is of great importance, since for the patient, it sets the pattern of all subsequent ones. The therapist will be aware that the patient has been anticipating what is about to happen with considerable apprehension. It is likely that he will have turned over in his mind the answers to many of the questions which he expects to be asked.

The patient is welcomed into the room and shown to his chair. If necessary he is relieved of his luggage and outdoor clothing. The therapist may offer an ashtray as an indication that he may smoke. He does not offer him a cigarette.

When both are seated, the main identifying points should be checked: the patient's name, his address, his telephone number, his age and occupation, his marital status and the name and address of his own doctor. If the therapist is a psychiatrist, he should make this clear at the outset. Then a fairly general opening question should be put. He may, for example, be asked 'What was it that took you to your own doctor?' or 'What was it that led you to seek help?' When it is appropriate, the patient may be asked how he feels about coming for a *psychiatric* interview. The therapist should not ask 'What is the matter?' (for that is what the patient has come to find out) or 'Tell me what I can do for you?' (The possible answers to this question make the imagination boggle!)

Having put the question, the therapist must *wait* for the reply. Not infrequently the patient's mind goes quite blank at this point. Often he needs time to marshall his thoughts. Perhaps he immediately finds himself in the grip of a powerful emotion. The therapist indicates by his relaxed attention that he understands the ordeal which faces the patient, that there is adequate time, without any need to hurry, and that the therapist is not disturbed by the patient's immediate difficulty in presenting his problem.

In these early minutes, the patient may give various clues as to his anticipations, his apprehensions, his hopes and his fears. He should be allowed to tell his story in as much detail as he wishes. If it seems that the session will be finished before he has had time to finish, he should be warned of this about three-quarters of the way through, but he may be assured that he will be able to continue at the next visit. The patient tries to communicate the nature of his problem and of the efforts which he has made to solve it. He may indicate his opinion that he has done all that can be expected of him. He will almost certainly convey his expectation that a solution will be provided by the therapist.

It is worth recording some matters of fact. It is useful to know when and where the patient was born, and such details of his family as the ages and occupations of his parents and siblings. If any are dead, their ages, the approximate date and the cause of death should be noted. Were the deaths sudden or expected? If they were expected, at what point did the patient realise the relative was going to die? What sort of reaction did the patient have?

Similar information about his own family should be recorded. He should be asked the ages, the occupations, and state of health of his spouse and their children. How soon after marriage was the first child born? If it was conceived before marriage, what was the patient's attitude towards the pregnancy? How did the members of his family feel about it? If the patient is a woman, she should be asked the number of times she has been pregnant.

The patient should be asked about his school and employment record. What were his best subjects at school and which his worst. What examinations has he passed? How old was he when he left school? How many jobs has he held? What was the longest? What was the shortest? Why did he leave? Was he ever sacked? He should be asked about his hobbies and his interests. How much does he drink and smoke? What about his physical health? Has he ever been 'in trouble'—i.e. involved in criminal activity?

At a convenient point, the therapist must enquire in detail about the patient's sexual experiences. If he is married, how has the sexual side of his marriage been? Has he been faithful? Has his spouse been faithful? Has he ever been tempted to be unfaithful? How did he resist the temptation? Has he ever had any doubts about the fidelity of his spouse? If there have been infidelities, does the spouse know about them? If he has been married more than once, what happened to the previous marriage? Does he have any other children? He may be asked, gently, about homosexual activities. When he was young, did he ever have a sexual relationship with a member of his own sex? Has he ever had any homosexual experiences in later life?

It may be helpful, especially in assisting the patient to express emotion, if the therapist enquires about the 'extremes' of his experience. What is the worst thing that has ever happened to him? What is the saddest, the most humiliating, the most shameful? What is it that has made him most angry? What is his happiest memory? What would be the worst thing that could ever happen to him? What is his earliest memory?

As the life history is outlined, a repeated pattern of behaviour may be perceived, and from this may be deduced some of the factors which have led up to the presenting problem. However, this does not auto-matically define the solution. Associations, similarities, and consistent patterns of behaviour may be observed and should always be discussed with the patient.

Sometimes the patient will remember episodes from the past which he had 'quite forgotten'. These will usually be found to fit into the basic pattern, and when this is accomplished, further 'forgotten' memories may be recalled. The patient may talk about things that are actually happening in the counselling situation. Frequently, he will be curious about his therapist, and may put apparently 'innocent' questions, such as 'Are you married?' 'Do you have a family?' or 'Don't you get tired of listening to problems all day long?'

When this sort of question is put, the therapist must consider with the patient its relevance to the problem which is under consideration. The patient may present a 'rational' explanation. He may say that the answers will give him confidence in his therapist. He may ask 'How can I trust *you* with a marital problem, when I don't know whether or not you are married yourself?' The implication is that he does *not* know whether or not he can trust the therapist, and that an unmarried therapist would be unable to help him. This point should be discussed carefully. The patient may protest rather hurriedly that he did not mean this at all, and the therapist's task is then to help the patient consider whether or not this is so. It is extremely necessary, but of course not always easy, for the patient to say things which may not be particularly flattering to the therapist. The therapist has agreed to listen to whatever the patient wishes to say. He is not concerned with flattery or disparagement.

At the first interview, the therapist should say something of what he expects from his patient, although it is not necessary to discuss the full extent of the 'contract' (see page 25). The therapist will expect the sessions to begin punctually, and the patient should be told for how long they will continue. He is expected to give top priority to therapy, but if circumstances make it quite impossible for him to keep his appointment, he must notify his therapist forthwith. He can be told that he may *say* anything, and that he should not evade topics on the grounds that they are embarrassing, shameful, disloyal, distasteful, or because they appear to be irrelevant. He may *say* anything he likes. He may *do* only that which would be acceptable in any professional relationship.

Replying to letters

The therapist is advised against getting into prolonged *correspondence* with patients. If he receives a letter he should acknowledge it but indicate in his reply that the points raised should be dealt with at the next meeting. He should refrain from answering specific topics in the letter itself.

Duration and frequency of sessions

The therapist should decide for himself the duration of his sessions. The length may be whatever is appropriate for his method of working. However, certain limits are suggested.

Generally speaking, sessions should last for at least 30 minutes. The maximum length is 60 minutes. A session which lasts for less than 30 minutes scarcely has the opportunity of beginning before time has come for it to finish. Sessions lasting more than 60 minutes are really too long for either the patient or the therapist. Some patients are very willing to embark upon marathon sessions which may last for several hours, but this is far beyond the attention-span of most therapists. Furthermore, this sort of practice deprives the patient of the many valuable periods of reflection which occur between sessions. For verbalisation to be of maximum value, the patient requires time to contemplate what has been verbalised. The content of a 60 minute session is quite sufficient for this purpose. Many therapists allocate a maximum time of about 50 minutes for each session, which allows 10 minutes between patients, five at each end of the hour. Joint sessions require a rather longer time: 90 minutes is usually adequate.

The therapist must remember that the work he does demands considerable concentration, and he himself needs adequate periods of rest. The ideal span of working time will vary with the individual. Most therapists require a rest of about half an hour, every $2\frac{1}{2}$ to 3 hours.

When intensive psychotherapy is practised, individual sessions should be as frequent as possible. Two or three may be required every week. In psychoanalysis, the patient attends for five sessions each week. When the frequency falls below once a week, the work is likely to be of less value, although in units where the pressure of work is great, there may be no choice in the matter.

Psychotherapy usually continues for at least six months. Twelve to thirty-six months is quite usual.

Emergencies

Occasionally a case is considered to be of great urgency. On other occasions the patient is important. The therapist may be asked to 'fit him in' to a diary which is already full. The wisdom of such a procedure must be questioned.

'Fitting someone in' usually implies that a brief consultation will be sufficient, but brief consultations—perhaps of only five or ten minutes—are of no particular value, either to the patient or to the therapist, for the interview is allowed insufficient time for any real momentum to be developed. If it shows signs of doing so, the therapist may be compelled to bring it to a premature halt. This may be especially so in the case of a true emergency. On the other hand, if the patient is given a full-length interview, the time must be taken from other patients. Even brief interviews are conducted at the expense of other patients. Therefore, it is rarely advisable to 'fit someone in'. The patient is best to wait until a proper consultation can be arranged.

In fact, true emergencies are rare in psychotherapy. There are times when the patient may feel an urgent need to contact his therapist, but this should be discouraged. He must restrict his contact to the appointed times. If he is being seen several times every week, it is unlikely that an occasion of such urgency will arise that it truly cannot wait until the next session.

Emergencies occur most often in dependent personalities and represent their imperious demand for instant relief. The development of tolerance, patience and self-discipline is an integral part of therapy and the patient must learn to endure a certain amount of discomfort and distress. The therapist must take occasional and calculated risks when dealing with his patients, just as one day parents must allow their children to cross the road alone. The therapist should indicate to his patient that he does not consider it to be in his interest, always to be stampeded by an angry demand for immediate succour. It is not pleasant and may not be easy, to be told that he must wait until the next appointment, and the patient may respond with anger, recrimination, or even blackmail. But when the first emergency has been faced successfully, it becomes easier to face the subsequent ones.

Use of Christian Names

Early in his professional career, the therapist must decide how he intends to address his patients, and how he wishes them to address him. Should they call him Doctor W or Henry? Should he call them Mr X or Arthur? Christian names are used in everyday life when a degree of intimacy exists between the speakers or when one is speaking to a child or to an inferior. But psychotherapy is not part of everyday life: it is a professional interchange of some complexity. The degree of intimacy which exists between therapist and patient is, because of the principle of anonymity, a rather one-sided one. Usually, the therapist expects the patient to call him by his professional name— to call him Doctor Y or Mr Z—although for rather specious reasons, some therapists invite patients to address them by their Christian names. They think that this will make them less formidable, and that it will be easier for the patient. But the dread lies in the therapist, not in the name by which he is known, and the author sees little of value in the practice.

The name by which the patient is called requires some discussion. In many centres, he is automatically called by his Christian name, whether he is 9 or 90. Presumably the object is to put him at his ease, but it also puts him on the level of a child or of an inferior. Neither of these positions is appropriate in psychotherapy. As far as possible, the patient is expected to act like an adult, and if this is the case, he should be treated like one. The younger the patient, the more important is this rule. Patients sometimes plead to be called by their Christian names. This is the psychological equivalent of their asking to be treated like children. The author's practice is always to address his patients in the same way that he expects to be addressed by them. The reader will undoubtedly feel that this is a matter for disputation.

Presents and Favours

It is not uncommon for a patient to offer a present to his therapist. There are times when it is very tempting to seek the assistance of a patient. When one is facing the purchase of an expensive item it may seem foolish not to accept a patient's offer 'to get you something off the price'. There may seem little harm, when one is having car trouble, to accept the offer of a motor-mechanic patient to 'put it right for you'. The therapist is advised to avoid all of these and similar temptations, for if he does he will, sooner or later, have cause to regret it.

If a present is refused, the patient may express feelings of being hurt or offended. He will plead that the therapist quite misunderstands the purpose of the gift. It is not meant as a bribe: it is merely an expression of his gratitude and perhaps of his affection. Often, it seems churlish to refuse. But the therapist should refuse nevertheless.

When counselling or therapy is completed, and if the patient particularly wishes, the therapist may suggest that he makes a contribution to the parent organisation or to an associated charity. He should not accept a personal gift.

7. Problems for the Therapist

CARDINAL PRINCIPLE: For some situations there are no cardinal principles.

Admission to Hospital

At the beginning of psychotherapy, or sometimes during its course, it may be necessary to consider the wisdom of admitting a patient to a psychiatric unit. This decision should be made only after the consequences of the step and its various symbolic meanings have been considered very carefully.

When a doctor tells a patient to come into hospital, the message he gives, in effect is this: 'You are ill. The situation is too complicated to be managed by your own people under your own roof. I will provide an alternative roof and other people'. But of course this may not necessarily be true. There are very few illnesses, even physical ones, which cannot be managed perfectly well in the patient's own home, provided that certain basic facilities are provided. However Britain is a hospital-orientated country. Beds are available (and must not be left empty) and it is often more convenient for the therapist to treat several patients together in one centre, than individually in their separate homes.

It is certainly easier to treat in hospital a patient who is acutely distressed. There, he will not disturb the neighbours—although he may disturb the other patients. The relatives of a patient who is suicidal may themselves feel more at ease if he is in hospital. Occasionally, where domestic friction has led to considerable tension, there may be something to be said for separating the antagonists. This can be achieved with dignity and without loss of face by arranging for one of them to be admitted to hospital. It is often rather a random matter to decide which one is to be labelled as 'the patient', and some units solve the difficulty by admitting all the participants together.

If admission is decided upon, the consequences must be faced. Of these, the most serious is that sooner or later, the people between whom the problem has existed must be reunited. It is probable that the 'patient' will be visited regularly, and that his partner will be interviewed, but their separation is an artificial one, and a time must come when they must return to the point at which they were parted.

Whilst he is in hospital, the rules of the culture will entitle the 'sick' person to sympathy, compassion and grapes, whilst his partner may have to accept the role of the villain of the piece. Many patients who are overwhelmed by hopeless distress when at home or at work, improve very rapidly once they are admitted. They feel 'safe' and although, with some vehemence, they may repudiate the idea, they prefer the role of a 'sick' person, who is compelled to conform to the demands and limitations of treatment, to the freedom, independence and conflicts of their own home. Such a patient may protest 'You don't think I *like* it here, do you?' As always, the answer should be 'Could it be possible that you prefer this place to your home?'

With certain reservations, the therapist may consider that it is appropriate to provide a patient with a temporary haven, but the procedure, which itself may solve *all* of the patient's difficulties for *some* of the time, is only a temporary one, and the first aim of therapy will be to expedite his return home.

Joint Interviews

Since problems always arise *between* people, it is often of value to see together the parties concerned. When this is possible the problem may be observed at first hand.

The procedure is as follows. A detailed account of the problem is taken first from the 'patient'. As has already been indicated, it is often a matter of chance as to which of the partners is called the 'patient'. It may be simply the one who 'cracks' first. Next the other partner is seen alone, and a detailed account is taken from him.

After this, the couple are seen together. They sit in something short of a semi-circle. The parners sit together: the therapist next to the patient or to the partner of the sex opposite to his own. The patient is asked to repeat his description of the problem as he sees it. He has, of course, already given a full account, and the therapist should insist that he tell of all its aspects, no matter how embarrassing they might be, or how difficult. As his partner hears this account, she may try to interrupt if it differs from her own to any significant degree. The therapist should gently but firmly forbid such interruptions. He will assure the partner that she will shortly have an opportunity of presenting her side of the case.

As he describes the problem to the therapist, the patient is also describing his view of it to his partner. This may be the first opportunity of doing so that he has ever had. On previous occasions she may have completely refused to listen to his point of view, or he to hers. Instead, one or other may have stormed out of the house, or have found some other way of evading any further discussion. Discussion may have been terminated by a threat of violence, or even by violence itself. In the consulting room, however, the couple have the unspoken fantasy that the therapist will be able to avert such an eventuality, although there may be no realistic justification for such a belief.

When the patient has presented his view of the situation, the partner is invited to describe hers. Once again, this may be the first time the patient has heard his partner's viewpoint. He too may try to interrupt when her ideas do not coincide with his own, but interruptions are again firmly but gently discouraged, until the partner has said all that she wishes.

It is at the next stage that discrepancies can be straightened out. Usually this can be achieved without any great difficulty. One partner will agree that he has overstated his case, or may confess that he has no recollection of a particular incident. His recollection may be only a dim one. Occasionally it will have to be accepted that a difference cannot be reconciled, and when this happens the partners must acknowledge that they see the event through different eyes.

During the course of joint interviews, it may be necessary to clarify certain basic points. Do the partners *wish* the problem to be solved? If they are married, do they wish the marriage to continue? The therapist must be willing to acknowledge that some problems have no solution. If this is such a case, what do the partners wish to do about it?

At the conclusion of a joint interview, it is probable that the partners will continue their discussion together, perhaps being encouraged to do so by their new found understanding of one another. The therapist will find that joint interviews are a rewarding and sometimes exceedingly productive form of psychotherapy.

It sometimes happens that two therapists are involved separately in the treatment of the two partners who have come upon a problem. They may then find it of value to combine to conduct joint interviews. When this approach is chosen, it should be decided in advance which therapist will open and which will close the session, and what particular points should be covered. The co-therapists must work together closely, and must spend some time, both before and after each session, discussing each other's contribution to therapy. The system is expensive of therapist-time, but provides the invaluable experience of learning about one's own technique through the medium of the co-therapist, who observes the mode of working of his colleague without appearing to be unduly intrusive.

A problem sometimes exists between more than two people. It may exist between two or more *groups* of people. The method of joint or multiple interviews is equally applicable in such cases, and the outcome is often gratifying.

Information from friends and relatives

It may happen that friends, relatives, employers, neighbours, workmates or other people who know the patient well will offer information about him which they consider to be important. This information may be accepted on two conditions. The first is that the therapist should be free to tell the patient what has been discussed. Information offered under a pledge of secrecy is of no value whatsoever and must never be accepted. The person who wishes to impose such a condition may be asked why such secrecy is necessary. Often it is because he expects a violent or antagonistic response from the patient. Such fears are usually quite unjustified. A therapist who nevertheless accepts information under a pledge of secrecy places himself in an invidious position, for it may truly be of importance, but he is unable to use it. When the difficulties are explained to the informant, and his own apprehensions are discussed, the need for the pledge (like other problems) often dissolves away, and the information can then be received unconditionally. If a pledge is still demanded, it should not be given. The informant should be told to think the matter over. If he is prepared to supply the information without such a promise, he can get in touch with the therapist at a later date. Very often he does so.

A person who wishes to give information about a patient should not be seen without the prior knowledge and consent of that patient. This is really an extension of the rules about confidentiality (q.v.). The therapist who agrees to see an informant without his patient's consent is risking the development of a situation of secrecy, and he will probably regret it. If the patient will not give his consent for the therapist to talk to the informant, the reasons should be examined. They may disappear when this is done, but the patient's decision must be respected, whatever it may be.

Confidentiality

Patients frequently ask with some anxiety, 'This is confidential, isn't it?' When such a question as this is put, the therapist's first task is to consider with his patient, what would it be like if others were to know? Patients often have elaborate fantasies in which they imagine that even their most innocent behaviour will be of enthralling interest not only to their nearest and dearest, but also to their townfellows, their countrymen, and occasionally even the whole world. They suspect that if others were to have the slightest inkling of their problems, they would be the subject of scorn and derision wherever they went. Grandiose fantasies such as these must themselves be the subject of careful scrutiny.

Having dealt with the fantasies, the facts must be considered. In Britain, neither doctors nor counsellors of any other sort can claim privilege in respect of matters discussed by them with their patients, and if they are ordered to do so in Court they must reveal them. Privilege can be claimed by ministers of religion only in respect of information which has been obtained during the course of confession. It is not possible, therefore, for the therapist to give an *absolute* guarantee of confidentiality. The patient will usually understand the reason for this. The therapist will however be able to assure the patient that normally he will respect the privacy of what he hears, and that he will not disclose it except by virtue of quite exceptional reasons.

Circumstances may occur in which the need for a breach of confidentiality must be considered. For example, the therapist may hear of a criminal act, either contemplated or completed, and obviously careful thought must be given to the problem of whether or not such information can be kept secret. In general, the public good is considered to outweigh the rights of the individual, and where ethical problems arise, the therapist must consult with senior colleagues or professional advisers before making his decision. It is nevertheless his own. The doctor should consult his defence union, the worker in a voluntary counselling agency should consult the agency's legal adviser, and so on.

Another point about confidentiality concerns the question of to whom the information should be considered confidential? If the therapist is working in a hospital, does the information belong to him or to the hospital? Should a junior doctor be free to discuss confidential information with a senior colleague? If a counsellor belongs to a voluntary counselling organisation, does the information belong to him or to the agency? If the therapist leaves the district, may the information obtained by him be passed on to his successor? If the patient leaves the district and is treated by a new therapist, may the new therapist have access to the notes of the old one?

Generally speaking, it is best to consider that the information is confidential to the organisation for which the therapist works. But there are some exceptions. It is obviously not desirable that information confided by an employee to his welfare officer (who is also an employee) should belong to the organisation for which they both work. The subject raises other problems, and there may be times when the therapist can do little more than assure his patient that he will respect his desire for privacy as far as he can. Absolute confidentiality can not, and should not, be guaranteed.

Scapegoating

In our culture very few people are prepared readily to accept responsibility for their mistakes. Errors of commission or omission are nearly always blamed on to someone else, or ascribed to the vagaries of inanimate and defenceless objects such as computers. Blame may be laid at the foot of government departments or the nationalised industries. Pride of place on the list of accepted scapegoats must surely be given to the postal services, which, more often than any other organisation, are unjustly blamed for the shortcomings of the people who forget to use them.

Scapegoating is a common device and in psychotherapy it is usually easily detected. Scapegoating is really a form of lying. The patient may be reluctant to acknowledge this fact, but he should be helped to do so.

Acting Out

Reference has already been made to the fact that the patient is required to express in words his thoughts, his feelings, his ideas and his wishes (see 'the contract', p. 25). If a patient endeavours to achieve this goal by other, more direct means, he is said to be 'acting out'.

For example he may wish to express negative feelings towards the therapist. He may do this indirectly, by going to another doctor and asking for a prescription for tranquilisers. He may do it directly, by being consistently late for his appointments. By making a suicidal attempt he may express feelings of being uncared for, so that someone is compelled to undertake his care. He may express affection for his therapist, by prolonging the handshake at the end of the session. All these are methods by which the patient 'acts out' his feelings either towards the therapist, against him or towards other people. They defy the spirit of the contract, in that the patient is expressing his feelings in behaviour, instead of in words.

'Acting out' should always be interpreted. The therapist may help by putting into words his own interpretation of what is meant by such behaviour ('It appears that you are angry with me: That you feel I do not care enough'. Or 'It seems that you feel very fond of me'.) Patients who persistently act out their feelings are usually unsuitable for intensive psychotherapy, and should be warned that therapy will be discontinued if the acting-out behaviour does not cease.

Joking

There are several jokes in this book. Joking may be appropriate in education, when it can be used to emphasise a point. Jokes are not appropriate in psychotherapy. The therapist is advised not to joke with his patient nor to respond to jokes made to him—seldom a very difficult matter. The patient may accuse the therapist of being cold and humourless, but such a statement expresses some of his negative transference feelings. He regrets that the relationship between them cannot be made into a warmer one. The appropriate interpretation should be made.

It may happen that a patient will present a serious problem of his own in the form of a joke. He may, for example, tell a story about homosexuals. The therapist should always examine such a communication in the light of 'true words are often spoken in jest'. It would be fatal to the relationship if the therapist were to fall into the trap, treating as a jest something that is deeply felt by the patient.

Second Opinions

If often happens that the therapist finds that he himself is in need of advice or guidance. Perhaps he feels that he is out of his depth, or that he is getting nowhere. Sometimes he would like an acceptable excuse for getting rid of a patient. Occasionally, a client complains to his counsellor of physical symptoms and both wonder whether these indicate the presence of organic disease.

When the therapist considers that a second opinion is desirable, he should first clarify for himself the nature of his own need. Too often, the request for a 'second opinion' is an excuse for the hope that one counsellor may be able to unload a difficult or unrewarding client on to the shoulders of another. If this should be the counsellor's hope, he need not shrink from admitting it, either to himself or to the person whose opinion he seeks. It may then be possible for them to consider together why such a situation should have arisen; whether it could have been foreseen, whether it can be changed, and whether indeed it might be better for the client to be treated by someone else.

There are certain occasions on which a second opinion *must* be sought—at least by the non-medical therapist. These situations are characterised by the development of a clear-cut *change* in a patient who has passed his mid-30's. The change may be in his physical health or in his psychological outlook. It must be emphasised that a *change* should have occurred. An individual who has been chronically anxious throughout his life need not usually be sent for a second opinion simply because he has passed his 36th birthday. A patient who, up to the age of 40, has been reasonably well integrated, and who then suddenly develops persistent symptoms of anxiety, for which there is no obvious reason, must be given the opportunity of a second opinion.

When the counsellor is working for a voluntary agency, the first source of referral should be to the client's own family doctor. The counsellor should never permit the family doctor to be bypassed. Sometimes the client will say that, for one reason or another, he does not wish his general practitioner to know about what is happening. Sometimes the counsellor will have a knowledgeable medical friend. Nevertheless, the general practitioner often has crucial knowledge about the client and his family, and in any case it is he who is ultimately responsible for the client's health. If the client does not feel confident in his own doctor, then he must find another. It is sometimes easy and convenient to bypass the general practitioner, but the counsellor is strongly warned against doing so. When the therapist is himself a medical practitioner, or is working as a member of a medical team, it is simple to obtain a further medical opinion if one is required. The therapist should always keep the general practitioner informed of the outcome.

When a second opinion is requested, it is advisable to *write* to the individual from whom it is being sought. The letter should be brief, should indicate the interest of the writer, and should describe the difficulties which have arisen. The letter should not be regarded as a device to demonstrate how clever, hardworking or well-informed, the writer is. If the counsellor thinks that, for example, a psychiatric opinion might be desirable, he may 'wonder' this in his letter to the general practitioner. He may not, of course, 'order' it. The counsellor should indicate his willingness to provide further information if it is required, and this may be offered either in another letter, or by direct discussion.

If the person who is to give the second opinion wishes to see the patient, the therapist should not try to predict what will happen' He should make no promises on behalf of the other person. He should not, for example, tell the patient that he will be expected to attend a clinic twice weekly for 12 months, or that a particular form of investigation will be undertaken.

When a second opinion has been given, the therapist must decide whether or not to accept it. He will usually accept it, but occasionally he may decide not to do so. When this happens he should explain his decision to the patient. It is *not* permissible to seek a third opinion, merely because the therapist disagrees with the second. To shop around for an opinion which agrees with your own is not seeking for a second opinion at all. To do this is unfair to the patient and dishonest to the person who gave the second opinion.

Use of Technical Words

A technical vocabulary is necessary for the exchange of ideas between specialists. It must be acknowledged however that people do not always use technical words in precisely the same way.

Certain technical words are adopted into the popular vocabulary, although not always accurately. At one time, poliomyelitis was commonly known as infantile paralysis. Now the technical term is almost universally used. Certain psychological terms like 'paranoid', and 'ambivalent' seem regrettably to be moving into everyday use: often in a careless and imprecise way. A word which may cause much confusion is 'schizophrenia'. In everyday speech, it seems to refer to the proposition that individuals may have varying attitudes towards a single object. Some people will say 'I am schizophrenic about Royalty', when they wish to indicate their opinion that the system has both advantages and disadvantages. The problem arises because schizophrenia is one of the most serious of psychiatric illnesses. It is not easy to describe. The layman often believes, incorrectly, that it is characterised by a splitting of the personality into two halves. In fact there is a *fragmentation* of the personality almost to dust. Consequently, if someone finds that he has a fluctuating attitude towards Royalty, or more ominously towards someone whom he loves, and when he reads in the newspapers that phenomena such as these are called 'schizophrenic', he may wonder whether he has the dread disease. Of course, if he has, his problems *may* be solved. No longer will he be required to take any responsibility for his actions. He may simply be confined to a mental hospital and looked after. Even schizophrenia has its advantages, (see 'Gain', page 58).

Another word which occasionally causes confusion is 'depression'. Its technical meaning is roughly the same as its colloquial one. However, since the development of effective treatments for depressive illnesses, the word is sometimes applied to other emotions as well. Nowadays, when a patient says he feels depressed, it may be advisable to ask him precisely what he means. 'Depression' can be used as a euphemism for bad temper, and it can even be used to describe people who are happy and cheerful. (Some drug companies have wallowed in the questionable concept of 'smiling depression'. This means that people who cry need antidepressants, and so do those who laugh! In fact it is never very difficult to detect a tear behind the rather watery 'conventional' smile of the depressed patient).

This tendency to use different words for the same thing, and at other times to use the same word for different things, can be the source of much confusion. It is necessary for the therapist to acknowledge that difficulties may be generated, and to make allowances for them.

When doctors are concerned, some apparent differences may cause considerable perplexity to their patients, who suppose that there is an alarming conflict of medical opinion when in fact there is none. In such circumstances the therapist may have to listen to terrifying stories of how doctors have differed, when he will know that probably there was no such difference at all. The patient may wish to ally himself with the view of the doctor he prefers, and to imagine that he is in opposition to the other.

It may be difficult for a therapist to listen to criticism of other doctors, especially when he is himself a doctor. He may feel that he must come to the defence of his colleagues, because 'there but for the grace of God go I'. He may feel that by failing to defend the other doctor, it will be tacitly assumed that he is joining the attack on him. Patients may reflect crucial aspects of their own personalities in their attitudes towards their doctors, and in the way in which they may express wholehearted admiration of one, or alternatively their very serious criticism of another. The criticism may not be spoken, but it is often there if the therapist is willing to attend to it. ('Dr A sent me to Dr B, and it was *he* who made the diagnosis').

When a patient criticises a doctor, the therapist need not rush immediately to the doctor's defence. The therapist's task is to help the patient say whatever he wishes to say, and if a patient feels that a doctor has acted badly, he should be helped to say so. The therapist does not necessarily agree with the criticism by this practice. At times it will appear that the patient's criticism is justified. Sometimes, by virtue of his personal acquaintanceship with the circumstances, the therapist may *know* that it is justified. However, these are relatively unimportant issues. The important thing is that the patient should be helped to say whatever he wishes to say. If there should be any undue sensitivity on the part of the medical profession in this matter, it is not relevant.

Short Cuts

Intensive psychotherapy and intensive counselling are prolonged and arduous procedures, and therapists frequently wish that there were some means by which the work could be accelerated. The patient, too, would prefer a speedier and less exacting means of securing relief. He will wonder whether he may be helped by hypnotism, by drugs, by prayer, by meditation or by such mystical means as yoga and acupuncture.

If it were possible to achieve quick and effective results by these techniques, there would be every inducement to employ them. Unfortunately, the high hopes that are usually held out for them rarely materialise. It would be very pleasant if everything could be resolved by the induction of a comfortable hypnotic trance. The patient would merely obey the commands of his hypnotist, and waken with all his problems solved. Unfortunately, the matter is far more complex than this. In the first place, the problem exists between people, so all would have to be hypnotised. A sonorous hypnotic assurance that 'You will no longer be frightened when your husband raises his fist to you' is rarely effective.

Similarly, the prescription of drugs do not solve the problems which exist between people. They may dull perception to some extent, so that less immediate distress will be suffered. It is very easy to advise a client to 'Get something from the doctor if you cannot sleep' but this is making a promise on behalf of someone else. The doctor may be of the opinion that it would be better to work out why the patient is unable to sleep, rather than to prescribe a chemical which will induce a state of unconsciousness, and also of dependence.

Tranquillising drugs and antidepressants have a very specific use, and they seldom combine with intensive psychotherapy. If a drug can do the job speedily and effectively, why bother with psychotherapy? Drugs are sometimes suggested as an 'adjunct to psychotherapy'. This is profitable for the manufacturers, but is questionable policy for the psychotherapist. If a change occurs, is it due to the drug or to psychotherapy? How can the therapist know that his patient's symptoms have not been merely suppressed by the drug? How can a patient be psychologically 'well' if he is unable to sleep without sedatives. If drugs are used, is the patient 'well' or 'ill'? Do drugs mean that there is a pathological disturbance to which the problem can be ascribed?

How much of a patient's problem is to be 'blamed' on to disease, and how much on to himself? If things go well, is the credit due to the drug or to the patient.

A procedure known as 'drug abreaction' is employed by some therapists. The patient is given a drug which alters his state of consciousness. A slow intravenous injection of a weak solution of Pentothal or Methedrine may be used, or the patient may be given ether to inhale, or nitrous oxide, or CO_2. In this way the patient may experience some reduction of his inhibitions, and may then express new material, or suffer a profound change in his affective state. When the procedure is finished, however, the patient may have little memory of it. He may say 'It was not me who said that', (or who felt like that)—'it was the drug'. The author's experience is that with patience, equal and generally better results may be obtained in clear consciousness, without the use of abreactive drugs. He does not favour the use of this method, although others find it useful.

The role of prayer and meditation depends on the circumstances in which they are to be used. True believers will often find help from their devotions, and such practices are entirely appropriate when the counsellor is acting under the aegis of a religious organisation. True unbelievers will find rational explanations of the alleged benefits. The author would not dispute that some people have found great help by such means. They are not, however, short cuts.

More mystical sources of help range from the sublime to the outrageous. The author is unable to believe that problems can be solved by sticking pins into various parts of the body, or by letting patients twist themselves into rather uncomfortable postures. He has no wish to argue with those who do.

Alcohol

It is not possible to conduct psychotherapy with a patient who is under the influence of an alcoholic drink. To make the matter absolutely plain, the author expects his patients to abstain completely from alcohol on the days on which they come for therapy. They may not drink until after the session is completed. Patients who disobey this rule are reminded of it, and the current session is then terminated. This may seem very harsh, but even a slight degree of intoxication reduces the value of psychotherapy, whilst states of moderate or severe intoxication makes it a complete waste of time.

The patient who disobeys the rule repeatedly may of course be addicted to alcohol. If this is the case, before psychotherapy can proceed, he will need assistance in order to stop drinking. When abstinence has been achieved, he must remain *totally* abstinent. Part of the psychotherapeutic aim will be to help him maintain this ideal.

The patient who is not an alcoholic but who nevertheless disobeys the 'no drinking' rule, is challenging his therapist. If confrontation is really more important than therapy, the therapist will have little hesitation in terminating treatment. If he drinks in order that he may gain sufficient courage to visit his therapist, the reason for this difficulty must be explored in clear consciousness. This may involve some hardship for the patient, and much self-discipline too. Such things cannot be avoided.

Sleep and Sleeping Pills

It is highly disagreeable to have to lie awake all night. The experience is one with which nearly everyone is familiar. It is even more unpleasant when insomnia continues for several nights, and one may then be tempted to ask for or to prescribe sleeping tablets.

Psychophysiologists who are interested in the problems of sleep in fact have great difficulty in keeping people *awake*! Even those who claim that they are unable to sleep for months on end, fall into a peaceful doze shortly after being connected to the leads of the electro-encephalogram (by which the onset and depth of sleep can be gauged). When they waken in the morning they exclaim triumphantly 'There you are! I didn't sleep a wink'. Usually they have in fact had several brief spells of wakefulness intervening between long periods of sleep. They remember the former, but not the latter. This is the reason for the conflicts which sometimes occur in hospital between the night nurses and the patients. The nurses report that a patient slept well all night: the patient accuses them of being asleep themselves. His *subjective* experience is that of being awake all night, and it need not be disputed that this is no less unpleasant for being subjective. The sense of tossing and turning, changing from one side to the other, listening to the hours chiming away, leads some people almost to the brink of desperation. 'I won't be good for anything in the morning', they cry.

But again, the psychological and physiological testing of people who are deprived of sleep shows that no notable fall off in performance occurs unless there has been a very considerable loss of sleep. So even this fear is without objective foundation.

The reasons for the subjective distress of 'insomnia' are complex. Some originate in childhood. Parents often attach great importance to ensuring that their children have plenty of sleep. Sometimes they send them to bed early 'because you are growing' but at other times, going to bed early is a punishment. Children often try to stay awake so that they can hear what is going on between their parents. Sometimes they fear bedtime lest they should see ghosts. Even fairly grown-up children, and quite a number of adults, are frightened of the dark. Some are frightened of staying awake because of what they may think. Others are frightened to sleep because of what they may dream.

Many of these difficulties can be solved (in one way, at least) very simply, by the prescription of sleeping tablets. These are cheap, effective and (in the prescribed dosage) safe. Since sleep is regarded as 'healthy' it may seem legitimate to request them as a means of securing health. The patient usually assures his doctor that he 'wants them only for a few nights' and that he 'doesn't want to get used to them'. But in fact, in Britain alone, the number of people who have got 'used to them' amounts to millions. The misuse of sleeping tablets represents a serious drug problem, and this has been largely created by the medical profession.

Sleeping tablets, like alcohol, are bad partners in psychotherapy. They emphasise the patient's dependence and fulfil his hopes that difficulties may be solved quite passively, the only effort required on his part being the ability to swallow. Sleeping tablets inhibit dreaming, so that this important means of access to the unconscious—to the 'Royal Road' as Freud called it—is obstructed. (A great increase in dreaming is regularly reported when hypnotics are withdrawn.) Finally, the *subjective* ability to sleep soundly is an important index of psychological health. How can the therapist assess a patient's wellbeing when hypnotics are being prescribed?

Two particular problems regarding sleeping tablets will be considered here. The first is, when can the prescription of hypnotics be justified; the second, how can they be withdrawn from people who are dependent on them?

Obviously it is appropriate to prescribe them, as a kindness, when a patient is suffering from a serious *physical* illness. It should however be borne in mind that some seem to *accentuate* sensitivity to pain, and then when the condition is a painful one, the prescription of an analgesic may be more effective. In psychiatric illnesses they should be prescribed only in *acute* conditions accompanied by marked and severe sleep disturbance: for example, in endogenous depression and in severe acute reactions to stress. Hypnotics should not be prescribed for a patient in order to ensure that the *doctor* can have an undisturbed sleep. The doctor who prescribes sleeping tablets should make himself responsible for withdrawing them at the earliest possible moment. The task should not be left to the general practitioner, or to another doctor.

The treatment of established hypnotic dependence is relatively easy, provided that one or two simple suggestions are followed. The patient may be assured that, although there may be one or two uncomfortable nights at first, when withdrawal is completed he will, within one or two weeks, be sleeping as well *without* his hypnotic as he was with it. He will probably be aware of increased (although not particularly unpleasant) frequency of dreaming. Within three to four weeks, he will be sleeping *better* without hypnotics than he was with them. Of course, if he has been taking sleeping tablets for many years, the first day or two of withdrawal are likely to *feel* extremely sleepless, and they will be experienced as correspondingly unpleasant. It is, therefore, a sensible idea to commence withdrawal at the beginning of a stress-free period: a long weekend is ideal for the purpose.

The patient is advised to confine his sleeping period to any selected eight hours of the day (for example from 11 pm to 7 am). If it has been his habit to take up to three tablets at bedtime, they may be stopped immediately. If the dose has been higher then this must be reduced first. In this instance, the process will take rather longer.

The patient should go to bed armed with an alarm clock set for the wakening-up time, a bedside lamp, acceptable reading material, a transistor radio with an earpiece, a thermos flask containing a hot drink, a hot water bottle or an electric blanket, and a convenient means of emptying his bladder.

It is sometimes helpful for him to take a hot milky drink before settling down (not tea or coffee!) Then he should wait to see what happens. He should not try to *make* himself sleep. If (as is likely) he finds himself unable to sleep he should, after a short while, turn on his light and read, or listen to the radio. When he feels like settling down again, he should first have some of the hot drink, and empty his bladder. He should ensure that he feels warm. He will sometimes ask if he can have the tablets at his bedside, to be taken if he is not asleep by a certain time. Since the object of the exercise is to discontinue sleeping tablets, the answer to this question is 'No'.

Very often he finds himself falling into a deep sleep just as the alarm clock rings. He may be tempted to turn over and to have another half hour in bed. But sleep is to be limited to the selected hours. So he does not have another half hour in bed. He gets up. Not infrequently, after lunch he feels like forty winks. He does not have forty winks. He is creating a 'physiological' sleeping tablet for himself and is saving it for the selected hours.

This simple routine usually works very well, and the patient's willingness to accept it in the early stages of psychotherapy may be a useful indication of his motivation.

Change

During the course of psychotherapy there may be occasions when the patient suddenly realises that all his problems will be solved if he divorces his wife, marries his mistress, sells his house, becomes a vegetarian and moves to Australia. But it is rare for problems to be solved by following impulsive decisions of this sort, and the patient should be advised to make no major changes in his way of life during therapy. If he ignores this advice, the changes are usually soon repented, and he finds himself without a wife, a home, a job, or even a corned beef sandwich.

Case Discussions

Whether the therapist is a member of a hospital team, or the counsellor is a member of a parent organisation; whenever periodic case discussions are held, they should be regarded as a *vital* part of therapy. It is part of the therapist's duty to his patient or client to attend regularly, and to take an active part. Such conferences are not to be regarded as an idle distraction from the real work of therapy, to be attended if time allows.

The ideal case discussion group has about eight members, all of approximately the same level of sophistication, and an experienced leader. It meets regularly, preferably every week, and lasts for about 90 minutes. Meetings must be given first priority by the members. Each takes it in turn, not necessarily in strict rotation, to talk about a case with which he is dealing. The case need not be one which has presented any particular difficulty. For preference, it should be presented extemporaneously, without notes or previous preparation. The members of the group then discuss the case, the role of the participants and particularly the involvement of the therapist. Sometimes they will endeavour to help him examine his counter-transference.

Such a group, meeting regularly over a period, can be of inestimable benefit to its members. They will help one another to become aware of some of the blind spots in their own personalities, and they will be assisted thereby to become more effective in their work.

Is it worth it?

There are times in every therapist's year when everything seems to go wrong. His patients seem to get worse rather than better—and lose no opportunity of telling him so. His colleagues complain at his incompetence, simultaneously sending him more and more patients. His car develops an expensive rattle, and his wife threatens to leave him, if he wants her to stand by him; or to stand by him, if he wants her to leave. Then, to crown everything, an eminent authority publishes yet another paper to demonstrate that psychotherapy is a waste of time.

The eminent authority usually compares two groups of patients suffering from neurotic illnesses. He is able to show that after a year or two, those who have had psychotherapy are no better off than those who have not. He thereby proves that neurotic illnesses follow their own course, and that psychotherapy makes no ultimate difference. The usual inference is that psychotherapy is a waste of time, money and energy, and that those who practise it are at least well-meaning simpletons, and at the worst, charlatans.

It has been emphasised several times that psychotherapy is an arduous and time-consuming procedure, so that in fact such criticisms as these must be taken very seriously indeed. If it is really a complete waste of time and effort, then practising psychotherapy should certainly be abandoned. The reader will however appreciate that the question is very far from being settled.

The first point to be made is this. In medicine, the physician is concerned as much with the means to the end, as to the end itself. Most people would make a complete spontaneous recovery from pneumonia. Antibiotics are not withheld on this account. Fractures could be reduced without anaesthesia. A patient suffering from agitated depression will recover spontaneously, without the use of E.C.T. or antidepressant drugs. It is the aim of medical treatment to speed the process of recovery, to minimise discomfort whilst spontaneous recovery takes place, and to make life endurable when no cure is possible. If psychotherapy serves any of these purposes, its value is assured.

Unfortunately it is often difficult to see how adequate comparisons can be made. How *can* the discomfort experienced by one patient during the course of a neurotic illness be compared with that endured by another? How *can* the distress suffered by people suffering from similar physical illnesses be compared? The questions do not appear to have a great deal of meaning. It must be agreed that the distress of certain *physical* illness can sometimes be alleviated by psychological measures, such as compassion, concern and tenderness, and that apparently some forms of psychiatric illness can also be alleviated by psychological means.

The crucial difficulty is that of measurement. Some psychological variables (for example, the I.Q.) can be expressed numerically but even then, comparison does not really mean a great deal. What can really be inferred from a statement that two men have I.Q.s of 75 and 150 respectively? In the measurement of personality, many other factors have to be taken into account. Ingenious attempts are constantly being devised to measure them but they present great technical difficulties, and the available techniques are still in their infancy.

However, the 'Is psychotherapy of any value' controversy continues to excite attention, and in so far as it encourages research into the measurement and comparison of personality it is of considerable value. One day, a satisfactory answer may be forthcoming.

Until that day arrives, many practising physicians will feel that the only worthwhile guide is what the patient says and does. He seeks help and usually he perseveres with it. No-one can say what would have happened if he had not sought help or had not persevered with it. For whatever reason, he feels himself to be better off with it than without it. Objectively, and at the end of the day, he might be equally well off without a therapist. No-one seriously behaves as though they think that this is really true.

8. Patients with Difficult Problems

CARDINAL PRINCIPLE: 'Tell me about it.'

The Management of Sexual Problems

Certain problems seem to cause as much anxiety to the therapist as they do distress to the patient. This may particularly be the case when a sexual problem is presented.

The patient who complains of a sexual difficulty sometimes precipitates a reaction of near panic in the doctor, who frequently responds, 'I am not trained to deal with this sort of thing. You must see a psychiatrist'. Then he hurriedly pens a referral letter. We must consider the wisdom of this procedure.

What must it be like, to be in the patient's position? He has a problem. It is an extremely personal one: a matter of great delicacy, which involves things about which he is deeply worried: perhaps something of which he is seriously ashamed. Some people might say that there are lots of people, in the world, like him—that there is nothing of which he need be ashamed. Nevertheless he is ashamed. He is embarrassed, anxious and frightened. He wonders to whom he can turn. Certainly he will be very careful in his choice of confidant. It will probably be someone whom he knows slightly, someone whom he respects, someone in whom he feels able to place some trust. Perhaps, of everyone in the whole world, there is only one person in whom he feels able to confide, so he seeks out that one person. Perhaps it is his doctor.

Sadly, doctors do not know everything. Their training does not cover all aspects of living. Furthermore there are certain things which interest them and others that do not. There are some topics with which they can deal competently and confidently, and others of which they feel ignorant or inadequate.

Very many doctors feel that they are 'not trained' to cope with the sexual problems of their patients. Often they too are embarrassed by them. Consequently, when a sexual problem is presented, the doctor's first thought is often to pass the patient on to someone else, as quickly as possible.

The 'someone else' is usually a psychiatrist. There is no particular reason for this. He is seldom better 'trained' to help with sexual difficulties than are his colleagues. It is true that he may have learned to be a little less shy when asking questions about sexual matters. But what about the patient? After weeks, months, maybe years of worrying, he finally decides to seek help. His mind is likely to be in a turmoil of anxiety. What is he to say? What questions will he be asked? What will he be told to do? For several days before the dreaded interview, he may become so anxious that he is unable to sleep. Eventually the time comes, and, frightened and embarrassed, he begins his tale.

Doctors often forget what it is like to be a patient—unless they become patients themselves. They forget the fear, the anxiety, the apprehension, and the rehearsal which precedes a consultation. They do not appreciate how profound is their effect on their patients. So how must the patient feel when the doctor whom he has selected with such great care, replies, 'You had better see a psychiatrist'?

The patient probably knows little or nothing about psychiatrists. He has some vague ideas about them, mainly derived from television and the newspapers. They are rather odd people, sometimes themselves a little mad, often little better than the people they claim to treat. They assist criminals to evade punishment, by saying that they are ill. They have extraordinary ideas about little boys being in love with their mothers. They are not quite respectable.

So when, with his heavy burden, the patient is told 'You should see a psychiatrist' often he *does not go*. What is more, he fears to consult anyone else lest he should be given the same advice. In consequence, his problem remains a secret anxiety affecting his whole life, perhaps even turning him into a chronic neurotic invalid.

It is, therefore, advised that the guiding principle in the management of sexual difficulties is this: *in the first instance the person to whom a sexual problem is confided should be the person who handles it*. He should not try to pass the patient on to someone else. He must say 'Tell me about it'. He should listen to the response. He must try to understand, however, alarmed, unsure or confused he may feel. At the end of the session he must ask the patient to return.

With surprising frequency, and as so often happens, the mere *verbalisation* of the problem may lead to its resolution, so that when the patient returns, he will sometimes say that things are a little easier. Almost certainly he will have had further thoughts and recollections to add to what he has already told. Three or four sessions of this sort may be all that is required to resolve the problem. When this happens the doctor may feel that he deserves very little of the credit, for it is true that much of the credit for successful psychotherapy belongs to the patient. But the doctor can be assured that, by offering his attentive ear, he has made a significant contribution to the satisfactory outcome.

Of course, the problem is not always resolved as easily as this, and after a few sessions the doctor may truly feel himself in need of more expert assistance. The specialist to whom he will usually turn is probably a psychiatrist. But by this time, the patient has become used to talking about his problem. He no longer feels that it is a shameful solitary burden, for he has been able to share it with his doctor, and he knows that the doctor has tried hard. Now he may be much more willing to accept the suggestion that a psychiatric opinion should be obtained. His attitude towards psychiatrists may not have changed, but he will be more willing to accept his doctor's advice.

It is helpful for the psychiatrist to know that the doctor has proceeded in the way which has been described. To tell the truth, if the 'simple' procedure has not been successful in bringing about the desired result, it is unlikely that a psychiatrist will have any more success. Frequently he represents the final Court of Appeal. His task may be to say that the situation cannot be changed. The referring doctor may then wish to help the patient face this disagreeable fact.

Sexual difficulties are concerned usually with disorders of either the *direction* or the *strength* of the sexual drive. The normal direction of sexual drive is towards an adult of the opposite sex. Instead, the sexual drive may be directed towards the self (masturbation); to an adult of the same sex (homosexuality); towards something associated with opposite sex such as the clothing (fetishism); towards a non-genital part of the body such as the hair; or (rarely) towards children, animals, and so on. Heterosexual adults who are well adjusted may nevertheless display traces of such deviations.

Masturbation is so common, especially in the young, that it should be regarded as normal: indeed there are some therapists who would regard the failure ever to masturbate as abnormal. Masturbation has no damaging consequences, but the shame which is felt about it and the anxiety which it may cause, sometimes leads to difficulties. These are usually resolved rapidly when the patient discovers that the therapist is in no way alarmed about the matter.

Homosexuality is very much more common than is generally supposed. Four per cent of the males interviewed in Kinsey's classical survey were exclusively homosexual, and 37 per cent had had some sort of homosexual experience, often in their youth. Homosexuality can be regarded as a *variation of normal*. The relative proportion of homosexual and heterosexual drive that they posses varies in different people. Most are preponderantly heterosexual: some are preponderantly homosexual. A few people are both, in which case they may marry and have children, at the same time continuing with a homosexual relationship.

Awareness that his drive is homosexual dawns often only gradually upon an individual, and he may have a long time in which to adjust to the idea. It may cause few problems in itself, and since there are now no de facto legal sanctions in Britain, most homosexuals are content to accept their situation and to gratify it discreetly.

People who are heterosexual must realise that homosexuals may fall as profoundly in love as they, and may feel as deeply the anguish of rejection. The individual who is exclusively homosexual feels as much re-

vulsion for heterosexual activities, as the heterosexual does for homosexual ones. Homosexuals have no more wish to be changed into heterosexuals than heterosexuals have to be changed to homosexuals. In
the occasional cases in which such a change has occurred, it would be
presumptuous of the therapist to claim the 'credit', for it was probably
going to happen anyway.

The limits of psychotherapy in homosexuality was described by
Freud with characteristic kindness in his reply (written in English) to a
letter from the despairing mother of a homosexual. He wrote:

9th April 1935

Dear Mrs .....

I gather from your letter that your son is a homosexual. I am most
impressed by the fact that you do not mention this term yourself in your
information about him. May I question you, why you avoid it? Homosexuality is assuredly no advantage, but it is nothing to be ashamed of,
no vice, no degradation, it cannot be classified as an illness; we consider
it to be a variation of the sexual function produced by a certain arrest of
sexual development. Many highly respectable individuals of ancient
and modern times have been homosexuals, several of the greatest
among them (Plato, Michelangelo, Leonardo da Vinci, etc.). It is a
great injustice to persecute homosexuality as a crime, and cruelty too.
If you do not believe me, read the books of Havelock Ellis.

By asking me if I can help, you mean, I suppose, if I can abolish homosexuality and make normal heterosexuality take its place. The answer is, in a general way, we cannot promise to achieve it. In a certain
number of cases we succeed in developing the blighted germs of heterosexual tendencies which are present in every homosexual, in the major-
ity of cases it is no more possible. It is a question of the quality and the
age of the individual. The result of treatment cannot be predicted.

What analysis can do for your son runs in a different line. If he is un-
happy, neurotic, torn by conflicts, inhibited in his social life, analysis
may bring him harmony, peace of mind, full efficiency, whether he remains a homosexual or gets changed. If you make up your mind, he
should have analysis with me!! I don't expect you will!! He has to come
over to Vienna. I have no intention of leaving here. However, don't
neglect to give me your answer.

Sincerely yours with kind wishes,

Freud

P.S. I did not find it difficult to read your handwriting. Hope you will
not find my writing and my English a harder task.

Homosexuality often causes concern to parents if they learn of it in
their children, and great distress to spouses when they learn about it in
their partners. The consequence of such a discovery is that they must

achieve a total reorientation of their outlook. Some relatives ask for treatment of the homosexuality in their loved one. They see his 'perversion' as evidence of 'disease', but instead it is they who really need help. The relatives' response may follow the pattern of mourning (q.v.). First they deny that it could possibly be so (hence the 'solution' that it must be due to some sort of disease). Next comes a distressed acceptance that it *is* so, and finally the stage of restitution '... after all, many of the world's greatest men were homosexuals...'.

One of the principal difficulties of a homosexual relationship is that although it may appear to be firmly established, it does not have the stability of a heterosexual one. It lacks the (sometimes questionable) security of marriage vows, neither can the presence of children make it reasonably secure. It lacks support and encouragement from the culture, which, on the contrary, exerts pressure towards its termination. If the relationship is ended, the homosexual may find it more difficult to find a new partner than might a heterosexual.

Consequently, homosexual relationships are innately less stable than heterosexual ones, although the need for security is as great for the homosexual as it is for the heterosexual. Certainly, homosexuals often have great need for support and reassurance. They love no less deeply than their fellows, and if a relationship which is already precarious shows signs of breaking up, they may be driven to the edge of despair.

Disorders of the *strength* of sexual drive, particularly of its diminution, are common. Reduction of sexual drive is called *impotence* in men, and *frigidity* in women. Both partners are, of course, affected—a good example of the maxim that problems arise between people. There is therefore not much value in treating one partner without the other, and the joint interview becomes of great importance. The partners are seen individually at first, then together, and each is encouraged to repeat the substance of what he has already told the therapist. Even if they have been married for a long time, some couples still have difficulty in talking with each other about intimate matters. Part of the task of the therapist is to help them overcome this difficulty. A new found ability to communicate may then continue outside the consulting room.

Certain powerful emotions, such as anxiety, depression, fear and anger impede the development of a satisfactory sexual relationship, and when such emotions exist they must be examined, expressed and dissipated before progress can be made. The *attitude* towards sexual intercourse often differs in the two sexes: for the male it is usually an end in itself, whereas for the female it is often a means to the end of pregnancy. If *conception* is the wife's only desire, it will not be surprising that she becomes frigid when contraceptive measures are taken. It is usually necessary for the wife to love her husband if she is to obtain sexual satisfaction from him: the contrary is not necessarily true and many men may have a good *sexual* relationship with women whom they dislike, despise or even hate.

The need of each partner to please the other is important for both. A wife may feel that her frigidity is more than compensated for by the pleasure which she is able to give her husband: the husband may feel that his own pleasure is diminished if he is unable to bring his wife to orgasm.

Such matters as these, and anything else that they may wish to share, should discussed by the partners. The therapist's role is to encourage the exchange, with as little interruption or prompting as possible. He must watch for any attempt to evade or minimise subjects which are difficult, embarrassing or painful. Everything must be discussed openly.

It is conceded that sexual problems may sometimes prove insoluble. If this is so, the therapist must discuss in detail the choices which face the couple, including the possibility of separation. He need not endeavour to cement a marriage which is damaged beyond repair: when this is the case, the couple would be best to part. But there is much more to marriage than sexual intercourse, and the existence of a permanent sexual problem does not necessarily mean that the marriage must break up. On the contrary: if such a fact is faced honestly, many couples decide to remain together.

Alcoholics

There are three certain ways of insulting a man. These are by denigrating his wife, criticising his driving, and calling him an alcoholic. Of these, the label of 'alcoholism' is perhaps the worst, conveying as it does the picture of a drunken, bleary-eyed sot; maudlin, dishevelled, neglecting his obligations; a picture of pathetic contempt. In fact, this picture is far from typical.

Not all alcoholics accept the diagnosis, but those who do fall into two main groups: those who care, and those who do not. The ones who care have often a very low opinion of themselves, feeling almost that the popular stereotype is too good. Their low selfesteem has usually anteceded their excessive drinking, and the development of alcoholism merely reinforces it. They believe that they cannot be worthy of the serious attention of anyone, and that the only people to whom they can turn are those in a similar plight. This is the origin of the common belief that only alcoholics can help alcoholics.

Those who do *not* care are unlikely to alter their way of life. They see no cause to stop drinking, and they do not intend to stop. 'After all, it's a free country', they will say, 'and I enjoy it'. People such as these see no reason why they should not beg, borrow or steal in order to maintain their supplies; feel themselves 'entitled' to live on social security: and are not prepared to take any responsibility for their families. They are often quite content to play the role of an amiable drunk, and fail to appreciate that the joke can become excessively tedious.

Patients of this sort, quite uncaring, represent almost impossible therapeutic prospects. They have little conscience and no motivation to change their way of life. It is they who may present the popular stereotype of the alcoholic, but in fact they are very much in the minority.

The typical alcoholic cares very much indeed. He is often hard work-. ing and responsible—sometimes too hard working and too responsible. He sets targets for himself which he cannot possibly attain. He dulls his nagging conscience with alcohol, and in consequence finds himself even less capable. So he adds to his burden of guilt. He can find nothing of value at all in himself. As he becomes more and more aware of his dependence on alcohol, he depends more and more on alcohol to free himself of the awareness. He feels helpless, hopeless, feckless; a worthless drunk. He feels that there is no one in the world worse than he. If he were suffering from a venereal disease, he would at least be suffering from the consequences of an excess of daring do. But as it is, he is merely an alcoholic.

Excessive drinking is common in neurotic patients and the therapist may find that problems have existed long before he became aware of them. They may be revealed only after many months of therapy. The patient now has the additional problem of how to confess his 'indulgence' to his therapist—how to admit that now he has added the misuse of alcohol to his other difficulties. By now, the therapist is someone who has become very important in his life, and he wonders what his reaction will be.

Tentatively, he tests out the possible responses. Perhaps he makes a little joke about drunks—but he observes very carefully the therapist's response. Such a trap as this is a good example of how important it is to remember that there are no jokes in psychotherapy; that everything must be examined for its underlying meaning. For if the therapist laughs heartily, how can his patient ever tell him...?

As always, when the patient eventually confesses 'I think I have been drinking a little too much' the response should be an unstartled, 'Tell me about it'. There should be no condemnation, no reassurance, no advice, and in particular, the therapist must not be ready with an instant 'Of course you are *not* an alcoholic'. For this combines reassurance with condemnation, and indicates certainty in the face of ignorance.

It has already been stated that drinking and psychotherapy do not go together: neither do drinking and problem solving. If the patient is really using drink to help him with his difficulties, he should stop drinking: if he has become addicted, he *must* stop.

The details of the diagnosis of alcohol addiction will be found elsewhere: here it is sufficient to describe four groups of symptoms, each of which is pathognomonic of alcoholism. An individual who experiences one or more of them is an alcoholic, and he must stop drinking completely.

The first of the symptoms is the occurrence of episodes of amnesia whilst the patient is drinking. Usually he is not particularly drunk, and his behaviour appears normal to those about him. However, when he comes to review the events of the drinking period, he will find that he has little or no memory of them.

Attacks of shaking or trembling, sometimes accompanied by a vague sense of apprehension, and occurring some hours after the last drink, are also diagnostic. Characteristically the tremors occur on wakening in the morning, and are relieved by another drink. If they are not relieved in this way, an attack of delirium tremens (d.ts.) may follow. Delirium tremens is the third way in which the illness may be diagnosed.

The fourth symptom is a fall in tolerance to alcohol. The patient finds that he is no longer able to 'hold' his drink as once he could. Commonly, he blames this on to 'getting older'. In fact it is usually due to advancing alcoholism.

There are two major problems in psychotherapy with alcoholics. The first is that of helping the patient to accept the diagnosis: the second is that of how to help him achieve the required target of becoming totally abstinent. No progress can be made unless the diagnosis can be accepted, but acceptance may lead to a further loss of self-esteem which is already precarious. The patient may persist in denying and rationalising what is obvious to everyone else. If this happens, the therapist may invite him to attempt a simple diagnostic test: for example, to remain *totally* abstinent for a limited period—perhaps of four weeks. The patient will often accept this sort of challenge readily, but he is seldom successful. Sometimes he will claim to have succeeded in cutting down, or to have succeeded except perhaps once, on a very special occasion. But this means that he has failed the test, and the therapist is bound to make this clear. When he does so, he need not feel a triumphant sense of vindication. He must not say 'I told you so' or adopt a 'holier than thou' attitude. The test is not an easy one: indeed it is probably beyond the capacity of some therapists. For the patient the implications of failure are profound. Can it be true that he is an alcoholic? What will his friends say? How will he himself feel? Worst of all, if he is using alcohol as a prop, how will he manage without it?

The patient who 'cares' about his addiction often has an underlying neurotic problem which has hitherto been dissolved away in alcohol. In turn additional problems are caused by the misuse of alcohol, so that now he has a double burden with which to deal. If the therapist will bear in mind that the patient is of low self-esteem, and will follow carefully the ordinary rules of therapy—particularly that of being non-judgemental—he can help the situation greatly.

When a patient is addicted to alcohol he is usually unable to stop drinking without help. Alcoholism, therefore, is one of the conditions in which it may be necessary to seek in-patient treatment. Admission will give the therapist an opportunity to attend to the patient's physical health, which may have been considerably impaired by continued reliance on alcohol as his sole source of calories.

Alcoholism is an insidious, chronic disease and relapses are common. Alcoholics are subjected to the same pressures as non-alcoholics— and they may be more susceptible to them—so that if the tension is too much they may turn to the same source of relief as people who are not addicted. If this happens, the therapist should not be surprised or disappointed. A relapse must be accepted philosophically, in the spirit of 'a man who never makes a mistake never makes anything'. The relapse may be a valuable experience for both the patient and the therapist. It provides a dramatic demonstration of the need for ceaseless vigilance.

If he is to remain well, the alcoholic must remain totally and permanently abstinent. No deviation from this rule can be accepted. There are times when it may seem painfully unjust. The patient may plead, not unreasonably, that 'Surely I may have half a glass of champagne to toast my daughter on her wedding day'. However poignant the circumstances, the answer must be an uncompromising 'No. You may not have even a sip'.

The patient sometimes tries to extend the limits in other ways. For example, he may say 'Will it be all right if I take just one glass and leave it at that. I am sure I can control it. If I am wrong, I will not take any more'. But *control* is one of the major problems of the alcoholic. Alcohol does not facilitate control; on the contrary it impairs it, so that the worthy intention is twice damaged.

Alcoholics, especially those with neurotic conflicts, may respond very well to psychotherapy. They have a valuable streak of independence. Other neurotic patients may go straight to their doctor when difficult situations are encountered, but the alcoholic tries to do something for himself—to 'treat' himself with alcohol. The treatment is inappropriate and ineffective, and in time leads to more difficulties, but at least the patient has striven for independence. With the sympathetic help of his therapist he may use the same determination to free himself, not only from his other problems but also from his alcohol dependence.

Alcoholics should never be rejected as potential patients or clients, merely because they are alcoholics or because they have relapsed. If reasonable selection criteria are employed, they may prove themselves to be very rewarding prospects.

The Physically Ill

The urgent preoccupation of people who are responsible for treating patients who are physically ill seems to be to reassure them that there is nothing seriously wrong, and that a cure will be achieved without undue discomfort. In consequence these patients may never have the opportunity of telling what their anxieties really are. Their fears are often quite irrational and totally unrelated to the condition for which they are being treated. It is therefore necessary to listen carefully to what they may wish to say. As is so often the case, the mere act of 'saying' it; the mere fact that someone is prepared to listen without displaying undue concern or agitation, will go a very long way to alleviate the fear. Naturally, it is legitimate to reassure the patient who has a serious physical illness, but the therapist must clarify the nature of the reassurance for which the patient is seeking. It is not necessary to force unpleasant facts down the patient's throat: instead it is enough to listen to what is asked, and to answer as carefully (and probably as truthfully) as possible.

The Dying Patient

The author was once asked by a patient who was dying of cancer, whether he was dying of cancer. The author, frightened and uncertain, gave a dishonest reply. The patient died four days later, knowing that his doctor had lied to him. The author has neither forgotten the experience nor forgiven himself for it. *Verb.sap.*

The Bereaved

The bereaved are those who mourn the death of their loved ones. 'Mourning' is the name given to the process by which they are reconciled to their loss. The process of mourning passes through three distinct stages: those of denial, acceptance and restitution.

When someone hears of the sudden and unexpected death of someone whom he loved deeply, his first reaction is one of denial. The word 'denial' is used here in its technical and psychological sense (see page 47). The mourner may say 'It cannot be true. I was speaking to him only this morning. There must be a mistake. It must be someone else. Perhaps it is just a bad dream. I will waken and find it was all a nightmare'. These are means whereby the mourner tries to assure himself that death has not really occurred.

The bereaved person may have no *intellectual* difficulty in accepting that death has occurred, but he may demonstrate *emotional* denial. He says that he cannot *feel* that it has really happened, that he feels numb, or that he does not feel anything. Sometimes he finds himself able to take charge in a curious and unexpected way. He is able to comfort others, to make arrangements for the funeral and so on. The people around him may express surprise at 'how well he has taken it'. He surprises even himself. This is due to denial of the appropriate emotional response. 'Denial' was manifested dramatically during the widowhood of Queen Victoria. Her Consort's room was kept always as he had left it, and his clothes were laid out for him each day, as though he might return at any moment.

Denial protects the bereaved person from the second stage of mourning, that of 'acceptance', which may be exceedingly painful. Fundamentally the pain is emotional, but it may take on a physical form. When the death was preceded by physical symptoms, the 'emotional' pain may take a similar physical form in the bereaved. At this stage the mourner weeps. He may cry quietly, sob bitterly, or sigh heavily. He has no particular wish to go on living. He does not usually think of taking his own life, but indicates that death would be welcome to him, for it would take him to his loved one.

Acceptance and denial may alternate, particularly in the early stages of mourning. The mourner will momentarily forget that his loved one is dead, and intending to speak to him, turn to his chair. Then, abruptly, he realises his mistake. Sometimes he 'feels' a presence as he goes into the room: he may actually 'hear' the voice or 'see' the form of the dead person. Frequently he may have vivid dreams about the deceased, but to his distress and dismay, these are not happy ones but horrible nightmares. He may dream that he is overjoyed by the death, and that he is laughing and singing over the grave. He may dream that he has himself killed the loved one. Such dreams usually cause great distress. 'Why' he pleads 'should I dream such things. I have never felt like that in my life.' (The reader should ponder over the answer to this question, bearing in mind that there is nothing so absurd that it can be dismissed without consideration.)

After death, a formal funeral ceremony is usually held. Relatives and friends gather together. Some have little acquaintance with the deceased, and the more distant relatives may have no particular reaction to the event. Nevertheless, old enmities are forgotten, and the mourners endeavour to offer support and comfort to the bereaved. The *fact* of the death is often acknowledged by a ritual viewing of the body. At the funeral the coffin is lowered into the ground, (symbolically, when cremation has been chosen) words of inevitability are spoken ('Dust to dust, ashes to ashes') and some of sympathy.

The pain of grief may continue for very many months. Every week of the first year brings some sort of anniversary. The people surrounding the mourner may be baffled and are uncertain how best to comfort him. Such phrases as 'It might have been worse', 'At least he did not suffer' or 'Now he is at peace' are shown for the empty platitudes that they are. People are sometimes disturbed to find themselves becoming angry with the mourner. 'Life must go on' they protest, or 'You really must pull yourself together—for the sake of the children as well as for your self'. Nevertheless, the mourner remains preoccupied with his loss. Why did it happen? Could it have been avoided? How might it have been foreseen? He may blame himself, over and over again. 'If only I had acted differently...' is the recurrent theme of this phase.

A time comes when the tenor changes. Life really must go on. 'He would want me to continue in the way he had begun...' This stage is called restitution. The loved one now becomes idealised. His faults are ignored or forgotten, his virtues acclaimed. One does not speak ill of the dead. The mourner takes up the reins again—often in the way which he believes the loved one would have wished. Not infrequently he adopts the mannerisms, the gestures, even the mode of speech of the beloved.

This three stage response to a serious loss is seen in many other forms in psychotherapy. What has been described applies to the case of a sudden death, for which the mourner is unprepared. When the death is a slow and lingering one, the mourner may have had months of preparation. Then, mourning begins when the mourner *realises that the loved one is going to die*. It is as though death had occurred at *that* point. The mourning process may be reinstated if the therapist asks, 'At what point did you realise he was going to die?' If realisation has occurred long before death, the work of mourning may be largely completed when death actually occurs. When it comes, the work of restitution has already started. The mourner may truly say 'It was a blessing. He had suffered so much and complained so little.'

So far we have spoken of death. But other losses must also be mourned. Such losses usually lead to a similar progression of denial, acceptance and restitution. A sick person may mourn the loss of a part of the body, such as a limb, a breast, the womb, or part of the stomach. Doctors assume rather too easily that, because an organ is an internal one, it has little significance to the patient: they should instead appreciate that the loss of an invisible organ may be very important to the patient. There are other losses to be mourned, too; the loss of youth, of vigour, of sexual attractiveness. There may be the loss of a job, of promotion prospects, or the frustration of ambition. There is the loss, through marriage, of one's own children. There may be the loss of a prized possession: perhaps one which symbolises a relationship. In all of these examples the loser says 'It cannot be so'. Then he must accept that it is so. Finally he will look for comfort in what remains to him.

The phases of mourning may be seen in psychotherapy, as the patient develops insight. He may have had an idealised view of some aspect of his personality for the whole of his life. In the course of treatment he comes to realise that he has deceived himself, and that he must abandon a favourite view. He may deny an interpretation heatedly at first, and will try to persuade the therapist to alter it. He may even threaten to withdraw from therapy. This is followed by the stage of acceptance. The patient becomes preoccupied and withdrawn, perhaps morose. His friends say 'That treatment is not doing you any good...you should give it up'. Finally comes restitution and reorientation: 'Well if that is how things are, I will have to do something about it...' By abandoning a cherished but false image of himself, the patient is thereby enabled to take a new, more realistic, attitude to his problems.

Suicide

When a patient encounters a very serious problem, and when other solutions seem remote, it is likely that he will consider the possibility of killing himself. If the therapeutic relationship is a satisfactory one, he will not be afraid to talk about such an eventuality with his therapist, who in turn will not wish to ignore such a preoccupation.

Certain points about suicide can be made straight away. The first is that at some time or another, nearly everyone has wondered— perhaps only momentarily—whether it is worth while to go on living. Would it not be better to be dead? Therapists, and especially counsellors, are often frightened to ask their patients about suicide 'in case it puts the idea into their mind'. Indeed some patients actually say, 'I hadn't thought about such a thing until you mentioned it'. In fact it is very difficult to 'put something' into someone's mind when its is not already there—or at least very nearly there. The therapist must never evade the question, purely for this reason. It is one of many difficult things which must be considered with complete frankness between therapist and patient.

Many therapists prefer to lead up to the crucial question fairly gently. They ask 'Have you ever felt that you didn't want to go on? Have you ever felt that life isn't worth living? Have you ever thought that you might as well be dead? Have you ever thought of taking your own life; of committing suicide?' The word 'suicide' must be used ultimately. (Note that these questions are put in the 'specific' form, since a committed answer is required.) The therapist should not fear to use the word 'suicide'. If he receives an affirmative answer, he should enquire precisely what thoughts the patient has had, whether in fact he has formulated any plan to take his life, and what active steps he has taken to implement them.

Sometimes, the patient responds to a question about suicide before it has been put. He may say 'I hadn't thought of suicide, if that is what you mean'. If the therapist has not used the word 'suicide', the patient's statement seems to indicate that he has thought of it. When the question of suicide is actually put, the patient may respond in several ways. He may weep, and confess that he has thought about it. He may pause for a while, then say, thoughtfully 'Well, no... but...'. He may become heated, and vehemently refute any idea of the sort. He may respond in a quite unemotional way, which carries with it a sense of reassurance, that indeed the idea has not occurred to him as a serious possibility.

As always, the reply must be attended to very carefully. 'Just talking about it' often considerably reduces the possibility that suicide will be attempted.

A 'successful' suicide has a profound effect on those who are close to the victim—to his relatives and, of course, to his therapist. Often they feel shocked, sad, and self-reproachful. Sometimes they are angry. They will wonder how the tragedy could have been averted. They will examine their own behaviour, and consider where they went wrong. Not infrequently they may endeavour to shift the burden of their guilt to the shoulders of someone else.

The person who considers suicide thinks carefully about the effect it will have on others,* and if he thinks that he can manipulate a desirable outcome he may subject himself to a situation of considerable danger. The angry lover may take a small overdose of a drug, not really to kill herself, but to bring her partner to heel. This suicide attempt, or 'para-suicide' has sometimes been described as a 'cry for help'. It would often seem equally appropriate to call it a 'scream of rage'. Although death is not intended, something may go wrong. People sometimes die 'unintentionally'. So even an apparently trivial episode must not be ignored.

On the other hand, an attempt at suicide may be very serious indeed. The reasoning seems to be as follows: 'Either I will die, when it won't matter; or the others involved will be so distressed that they will *have* to do something'. This attitude has been compared with the game of Russian Roulette, in which life or death is staked on the spin of the barrel of a revolver.

The counsellor or the therapist who is dealing with a patient who professes strong preoccupations with suicide, may find himself in a dilemma of considerable ethical and emotional proportions. Should he accept the gamble that the event will not happen? Should he reassure himself that 'people who talk about it seldom do it'? Sometimes they do, and the maxim—which is still commonly believed—is a reassurance, not a guarantee. Should the counsellor at once say 'Then you must see a psychiatrist'? A panicky response of this sort is no more appropriate to a confession of suicidal thoughts than it is to an admission of sexual problems (see page 95). As always, the better response is, 'Tell me about it'. Once again, the person to whom suicidal thoughts are confessed should be the person who, in the first instance, handles the case. Of course, he will feel great pressure upon him, probably greater than in any other situation, and if he is inexperienced the therapist may wish to consult a more experienced colleague. But no-one can predict with certainty what will happen. In some cases it may be considered necessary to take the patient's freedom away from him: to admit him to a psychiatric unit, in which he may be carefully observed. Even then there is no guarantee that he might not take his life. Alternatively the risk may be taken, and sometimes the gamble is lost.

*'I'll just die, then you'll be sorry...' (one of Ronald Searle's schoolgirls, crossed in love).

The final decision will be based on an assessment of the balance of probabilities. If it is decided that the patient should be admitted to hospital, the therapist may be forced to pass the case on to someone else, and much of his own work will seem wasted. The patient may regard such a decision as evidence of a serious breach of faith on the part of his therapist. Alternatively, the therapist may decide to ride out the storm—only to lose his patient.

Suicide is not a common occurrence when a patient has a close continuing relationship with his therapist. It is much more common if such a relationship is absent. However, it provides a point of anxiety and uncertainty for the therapist which can never be completely removed.

9. Problems with Difficult Patients

CARDINAL PRINCIPLE: Don't judge a book by its cover.

The Difficult Patient

The phrase 'difficult patient' is often a rather evasive euphemism for
a 'troublesome patient'. Although he may be suffering from a 'real'
illness, (whatever the other sort may be) he does not behave in a way
which might be expected of an Englishman and a gentleman. He may
in fact be neither, but that is not the point. He does not *behave* like
one. He muddles his appointments, insults the nursing staff, threatens
the receptionists and insists on seeing the head doctor. He is continually
telephoning about something or another, writes long and indecipher-
able letters, fusses about innocent investigations and makes a general
nuisance of himself. He does not seem to appreciate that investigations
take time: that emergencies must be dealt with first: that he is not the
only person who is sick: or that the doctors cannot perform miracles.
As a punishment he is sometimes referred to a psychiatrist, but psychiatrists are often worse at handling troublesome patients than
members of other specialities, and the referral merely adds to everyone's sense of grievance.

In an attempt to explain some of the behaviour of these people,
let us consider the chronology of their illnesses. First a symptom
develops. The patient does not know what it portends, and hopes
that it will go away. Perhaps he experiments with a patent remedy,
recommended by friends and relatives. However, he does not get
better and after a week or two he consults his doctor. The doctor
listens to the story, sometimes makes a cursory examination and gives
him a prescription. He tells him to come back next week if he is not
better. Sometimes he is cured, and the doctor takes the credit for
being a very clever man. But sometimes the symptoms continue. The
patient returns, and is given a different treatment. This does not work
either, and the doctor decides to refer the patient for a specialist
opinion.

Already several weeks may have passed since the symptoms commenced and it is becoming increasingly clear that no-one really knows
what is the cause. The idea of a specialist opinion is always rather
alarming. A whole week may elapse before an appointment can be
made: often it is more. The specialist listens to the story and says,

'Well, I will have to make some investigations. Come back again next week. We should have some results after that'.

So another few weeks pass by, and still the symptoms continue. The patient can scarcely be blamed for becoming progressively more alarmed. Then a point comes when he can bear the anxiety no longer, *'I want something done, now'* he explodes. From that moment on, he may be labelled a difficult patient.

Yet it must be very difficult to endure unexplained symptoms for several weeks, and not to become somewhat alarmed about their cause. Even the most sanguine might find their patience is strained, and when, as is often the case in these circumstances, the patient is not psychologically robust, the tension may well become intolerable. *The difficult patient is a frightened patient.* He will not be made less so by 'punishment', whether it is the obvious one of making him wait for a little longer in the queue, or the more subtle one of sending him to a psychiatrist. These responses are likely to make him worse, not better.

Then how should he be handled? Surely it will only make him worse if he is allowed to 'jump the queue'. Paradoxically, rather than making him worse, such a procedure will often make him better. There is something to be said for the practice of seeing troublesome patients sooner, rather than later. Their anxiety may be alleviated a little more quickly (to the benefit of the hospital staff as well as to their own!). By doing so, the staff demonstrate that they recognise the anxiety, and are quite willing to do what they can to alleviate it. And if, as so often happens, there was nothing to be anxious about anyway, he may be a little less frightened another time.

Doctors and their co-workers should always beware of refusing a patient's request *because of the way in which he makes it*. The reasons he gives may be the wrong ones, but there may be an ultimate logic in his request. A very immature woman demanded of her gynaecologist that she should be sterilised. She described her gynaecological history in terms of florid exaggeration ('...the flying squad had to pump *gallons* of blood into me...literally...there were seven doctors and they *all* said they had never seen such a *terrible* miscarriage. I can't *possibly* go through all that again...'). The demanding, importunate quality of the patient's presentation led the gynaecologist to decide that he would not sterilise her. But he had failed to appreciate that the attitude which she was displaying reflected the precise reason for performing the operation. By retreating into neurotic illness for months on end, the patient had completely failed to mother her first two children. Perhaps she realised instinctively something that was not immediately apparent to her doctor—that she could not cope with motherhood. Unfortunately she presented her request in the form of a self-centred, neurotic, *demand* of the difficult patient and on that account was rejected. After further consideration, it was decided that the operation should be performed. She then became calm and contented: perhaps not the most stable of women, but far less troublesome than before.

The Impossible

Impossible patients are impossible. There is no psychological technique which will make them otherwise. Some time may elapse before they are distinguished from the merely difficult, and it may be necessary for the therapist to face the fact that a patient on whom he has spent much time and trouble is such a poor prospect that all the endeavours which have been expended on him are completely wasted.

If a counsellor finds a client difficult, almost everyone else will find him difficult, too. There is no group of people, such as psychiatrists, who relish the prospect of managing impossible patients or who find them of particular professional interest. If he accepts a difficult client for counselling, the counsellor will not find it easy to pass him on to someone else if he has a mind to do so.

Clients such as these may be rejected for intensive counselling without difficulty, but it may be more difficult to refuse them supportive counselling. Certain organisations give the client a sort of 'right' to attention—for example, certain Government departments, such as the Department of Health and Social Security—so that outright rejection is impossible. Other organisations (for example, evangelical Christian ones) may refuse to acknowledge that there is any such person as the impossible client, and will always offer him some sort of supportive counselling.

Of course, people such as these frequently plead for help. They may be depressed, suicidal, hopeless, homeless and helpless. Their lives are in a mess. Often they have no job. They may be deserted by their families, move in and out of prison, and often depend more and more on alcohol. Women may indulge in prostitution. Sometimes they protest their wish to reform with apparent sincerity. They plead to be helped to make a new life for themselves, and it often seems unkind or churlish to regard them as impossible. They may show themselves to be unexpectedly tractable, and eager to conform to a new way of life which is pointed out to them. But the early promise is rarely maintained. A lapse occurs, which is confessed with shame and with remorse. A plea for forgiveness is made, and it is readily granted. Then comes a second lapse, then a third and fourth in rapid succession. How can such incorrigible people be helped?

They cannot: and paradoxically, when this is acknowledged, one or two of them may respond. Sometimes they seem to change when they are accepted for what they are, and not thought of as pieces of human clay which are to be remoulded.

Everyone carries a few patients such as these, but they are very wearing and only a limited amount of energy should be expended on them. If he agrees to counsel such people the therapist should accept only a limited number. The therapist must stand by his agreement. If he has made a mistake in his selection, there may be no-one who can extricate him from his difficulty. He may not pass such patients on to someone else, for this would be unfair to the patient and untrue to himself. He must accept his patient, even though he bitterly regrets his decision.

The dual discovery that he is accepted for what he is, and that no-one is trying to get rid of him, even for the most solicitous reasons, such as 'he is more experienced than I', sometimes presents a totally new and quite unbelievable experience to the patient. He may test his therapist out in various ways. He may get worse, perhaps even more incorrigible. He may endeavour to trick the therapist into dropping the case. The therapist who persists in accepting his patient as he is, despite these discouragements, and one who tries to share his world, may provide the impossible patient with a unique experience, which occasionally provides a point of true change. The therapist must not, however, expect any change, and he will not then be disappointed. If he *is* disappointed, then he can be sure that his original aims were too high.

The reader may be very dissatisfied with such diffuse advice as this: with the complete absence of any direct and practical way of dealing with the impossible patient: with the absence of any concrete suggestions which might have a chance of success. He may feel that what has been said is all very well, but that it does not apply to his patients. Surely there must be *some* way of helping them to see what a mess they are making of their lives, of making them aware of their responsibilities, of forcing them to behave in an adult sort of way, of getting them to understand that they must become less selfish.

Such pleas are particularly poignant when, as is often the case, the patient is young, attractive and intelligent. Then the therapist may feel especially that it should be possible to do *something*. Of course, as the patient becomes older, more dissipated, more obviously incorrigible, the pleas are muted, although the patient may preserve the ability to make people feel that he has been maligned and misunderstood from the start, and that he has never been given a proper chance.

The difficulty arises out of the fact that such people, although physically mature and of normal or even of above-normal intelligence, are retarded *emotionally*. Their *behaviour* is like that of tiny children. Like young children they are impulsive, self-centred and have little or no thought for the needs of others. They are unable to plan for the future, do not seem able to learn from their mistakes, and completely fail to understand mature concepts such as responsibility, industry and perseverence. Often, they seem to have no conscience. Their pleasures are usually simple—smoking, drinking, sometimes talking. Their emotions are primitive—unconstrained anxiety, or indescribable fury which may lead them to unrestrained agression. They do not really know what it is like to love or to cherish other people, although they usually expect undivided love for themselves. If they enter into a sexual relationship, they do so purely out of a bodily striving. Hence they are often promiscuous, and may be indifferently hetero—or homo—sexual. Needless to say, they take no responsibility for their sexual partner or for any children that they may father.

It is not easy for a 'mature' adult who has left such attitudes far behind, to feel his way into such a personality. The mature person plans for the future, learns from his mistakes and considers other people. It seems impossible to believe that there are adults who are so immature that they cannot understand such things. As a result the therapist may find himself unable to communicate with the patient on any meaningful level. Children mature spontaneously, not by being taught to do so; and the only hope is that ultimately the 'impossible' patient will mature too. This is a remote hope, but it is occasionally fulfilled.

It may not seem sufficient to say that these people are best helped by accepting them for what they are. Certainly, to accept them is much more difficult than it sounds. The therapist will often feel angry, frustrated and exasperated with them. At other times he will feel disconsolate at being able to do so little. He may wonder whether he might not be better to use his time more fruitfully, and whether he should leave the incorrigible patient to the experts. But the 'experts' are no better than anyone else at handling people like these. Probably, they already have a small burden of them, and they will not be enthusiastic about accepting more. If the therapist has accepted the buck, he may not pass it on. It is part of the price to be paid for the more gratifying forms of therapy.

Money

Most organisations have an immutable rule about money. They will help the client to manage what he has, but they will never, under any circumstances, lend or give him any. If this is the rule, it must be adhered to. The counsellor may be tempted to bypass it, sometimes, but he does so at his peril. Money and intensive counselling do not mix, and when such a rule exists, it is to everyone's advantage that it should be rigidly obeyed.

Some organisations offer a limited amount of money, food, shelter and clothing. When this is the case, certain difficulties arise. First the client's motivation may spring more from the prospect of financial gain than from the possibility of changing his way of life. He often shows himself to be remarkably well-acquainted with the parable of the Good Samaritan if the organisation is a voluntary one, and with his 'rights' if it is a governmental one. In the latter instance he is swift to point out how long he has 'paid in for it'. (Probably he has a totally unstamped card.) He sees no reason why he should not have it, if there is anything in the purse. If the counsellor endeavours to indicate that there are limits, and furthermore, that he is neither empowered nor prepared to extend them, he is likely to be greeted with surprise, reproof and sometimes aggression. In circumstances such as these, the problem of accepting limits is often a vital component of the client's difficulties. It is not to his advantage if the counsellor endeavours to extend them—even if he is empowered to do so. (Usually he is not). The best help that the client can be given is unpalatable. It is the clear demonstration that limits are limits. If this lesson can be implanted, the counsellor will have achieved a formidable success.

The prospect of obtaining money, especially state money, often brings out the worst in the client. He looks upon the counsellor as a sort of bottomless purse. He feels vaguely that he has a right to everything that is available: that he should receive whatever he requires, and that he is being unjustly deprived if he is not given all that he needs. Physical violence may sometimes be threatened, and if there is a genuine risk that it will be used, there need be no hesitation in calling for the help of others, such as the police, although in the long run this may make things more difficult.

A frontal attack is never of value in dealing with people such as these. The counsellor should remain sympathetic, firm and objective but he must be quite implacable. It is not worth getting into a verbal or any other battle. Sometimes it may be possible to divert their hostility to other, more constructive sources. The sort of thing that happens, stripped of embellishments, is as follows:—

The client comes to the desk, scowls horribly, and says to the counsellor behind it, 'Give me money'. The counsellor, who knows that he has already had his entitlement replies, 'You cannot have any'. The client becomes threatening. He says 'If you don't give me any, I'll bash you'. The counsellor becomes alarmed. His finger is poised over the alarm bell. He has several different choices of reply. He may say 'You can't have any'. But he has already said that. It would be best for him not to repeat himself. He may say, 'I would give you some, if it were within my power' (Would he?), 'but it is not. The authorities say that you have reached your limit'. But the counsellor and the 'authorities' are one and the same thing from the point of view of the client, and this reply is equivalent to an arbitrary decision not to give him any. In either case an argument may develop between counsellor and client, each operating on a different wavelength, and neither really understanding the other.

An alternative method is for the counsellor to 'feel' himself into his client's shoes, to try to imagine his feelings, and then to put them into words. The counsellor replies to the threat of being 'bashed' with the words, 'it sounds as though you feel angry' and the client replies

'I am! Bloody angry! So would you be, if you were in my position'. The counsellor must beware of reverting to the role of a bureaucrat. He continues to feel himself into the client's shoes, and replies 'It must be very difficult to be in your position. What is it like?'

The client then begins to realise that the interview is not going quite the way he intended, and indignantly he may try to get it back on to the right lines. He says, 'Look here, Jock,* I didn't come here to be psycho-analysed. Are you going to give me that money or are you not?' The counsellor points out that he has already answered this question, and that he does not intend to repeat it. The client baffled, changes his tactics. He says 'I can't get any bloody sense out of you. I'm going to write to the Prime Minister' (or to the Queen, to his Member of Parliament, and so on). The counsellor says 'Now, that's a very good idea indeed'. By saying this, he is acknowledging that the client proposes to do something on his own behalf, and he encourages him. 'You will get the address from the Public Library. Next time you come, let me know how you get on'.

The counsellor's task is to accept that the client is in difficulties, and that he is angry. He supports his proposition that there might be something he himself can do about it.

Many readers will say of this dialogue 'It sounds all very easy, but you don't know my clients. They are the most difficult people in the world'. It is certainly true that the writer does not know his reader's clients, but he knows people like them, and does not under-estimate the difficulties. But unless something of the sort is tried, nothing will be achieved. In fact it is not likely that anything will be achieved, but if just one or two clients carry out their threat, they will have made a beginning, and it will have been worth while.

Violence

The patient must not touch his therapist. This is part of the contract and includes the assurance that the patient will not offer physical violence towards his therapist. If he wishes, the patient may *say* to him, 'I am so angry that I am going to strike you'. But he may not *do* so! Obviously, no serious threat of violence can be tolerated. If the therapist should truly believe himself to be in danger, he cannot continue with therapy, and if it should be discontinued on this account, it can never be resumed again between the patient and the same therapist. Neither is violence towards other people to be tolerated, nor any activity which may be regarded as criminal. The therapist need have no hesitation in making this fact clear to his patient if it is necessary. There may be certain circumstances in which his public duty may override his ideals of professional confidence. Problems which are the proper concern of psychotherapy are not amenable to

*A different word is used South of the Border.

violence. If a difficulty should arise, the therapist may always consult his senior colleagues and, if they are available, legal advisers.

A special problem may arise if a patient is threatened with violence. In cases of this sort, the threat is usually beyond the influence of the therapist (except, for example, in marital counselling, when one partner may threaten the other). If a patient seriously believes himself to be in danger, the therapist will discuss the question of from whom he might obtain physical protection. The therapist cannot provide this himself, of course, and he should not be the one to ask others to provide it. The patient can ask for help from the police, for example, as readily as can the therapist, and if he thinks it is truly necessary he will not hesitate to do so.

Therapy Under 'Compulsion'

Here, two groups of patients will be considered. They have all been found guilty of a criminal offence, but the first group has accepted treatment in lieu of punishment, usually as a condition of probation. The second group is already receiving punishment and is detained either in prison or in some corresponding institution.

The patient who is receiving psychotherapy as a condition of probation may protest that he does not himself wish to be treated: that he is there only because the court has ordered it. Technically, this is incorrect. He has been offered treatment, and he has accepted it of his own free will. By virtue of his agreement, the court has agreed to excuse him from punishment. But although this is the *technical* situation, in reality the patient will feel that he has been 'sent' for treatment, for a choice between punishment and treatment is not really a choice at all. Consequently the patient often believes that treatment has been imposed upon him. In circumstances such as these, the patient's motivation is often seriously deficient, and treatment is seldom satisfactory.

This matter raises the problem of insight, and of treatment as a condition of probation. If a patient realises that he needs treatment, why did he not seek it before the offence occurred? It is difficult to avoid the conclusion that 'treatment' is usually thought of as a soft alternative to punishment. There are a few occasions on which the commission of an offence is the direct consequence of a pathological state, but these are rare. A housewife may have a severe depressive illness, and commit 'social' instead of 'physical' suicide by indulging in shoplifting. If the diagnosis is sure, it is appropriate to offer her treatment for the primary psychiatric illness. In the absence of strong medical indications however, the author advises against the offer of treatment instead of punishment. If there is doubt, it may be better for punishment to be imposed. If he wishes it, the patient can be treated after he has suffered punishment.

A patient who is actually receiving punishment is in a slightly different position. Psychotherapy, particularly group psychotherapy, is sometimes offered to selected prisoners. There may even then be a suspicion that these opportunities provide a welcome relief from some of the drearier routines of prison life. Furthermore, there are very few opportunities for the prisoner to put any new found insights into practice. In these circumstances, therapy is most likely to be of value in the cases where the patient undertakes to continue with therapy after he leaves prison. He will usually give the required promise to continue after discharge, but the failure rate is regrettably, although perhaps inevitably, high. Some prisoners hope that, by continuing with therapy after discharge, they will have a ready-made excuse for subsequent criminal acts. They may be warned well in advance that this is not so. Like everyone else, patients receiving psychotherapy are expected to conform to the law of the land, and psychiatric illness is not an excuse for breaking it. The courts are indulgent towards patients who are suffering from certain severe psychiatric illness, but the therapist will always expect his patient to obey the law.

Pastoral Counselling

The counsellor who is a member of a religious organisation is regarded by many of his clients as a man of God—as one of His direct representatives: sometimes even as God himself. Clients such as these expect him to behave without sin, and they will condemn any deviation from perfection. The counsellor may protest that he is only a man, just like everyone else, but his pleas are not likely to be heeded. He is firmly cast in a role, and he may have little choice but to accept it. Anything else involves fruitless, but not always spoken, argument. His parishioners expect ministers of religion to behave like saints, however inappropriate the role may feel. Anything which verges on the self-indulgent or which appears to be faintly sinful will be greeted by at least one parishioner with the reproof 'I would never have expected a clergyman to behave like that!'

The expectation that ministers should be perfect is not easy to tolerate, and the evidence is partly based on the fact that stories of fallen clergymen sell large numbers of newspapers. Knowing his own limits, it is perhaps wise for the minister, of all men, to adhere to Polonius's adage 'To thine own self be true'. The minister knows what behaviour is expected of him: he knows that it is sometimes very difficult to obey the laws of the Bible, and he himself must be willing to tolerate his own failures. Others will not find it so easy. Furthermore, he will discover, to his sorrow, that compassion and understanding does not cure everything, least of all his own problems.

In counselling, it is suggested that clergymen follow the general lines suggested in this book. They are, however, in the unusual position of being able to give advice, based on biblical authority, on how their parishioners should behave. Obviously they will not wish to depart from this authority, or to modify it in any way. They may concentrate some of their endeavours on how difficult it is for individuals to adhere to biblical precepts. When it seems appropriate, they will emphasise the ultimate Christian message of forgiveness.

If he is a member of a church organisation, the counsellor may, because of this, feel himself obliged to counsel everyone who asks for his advice. He may feel that he should never send anyone away, however unpromising they may seem, and that he must always be at the call of people who seek his help. This sort of outlook will be seized upon by a small but very troublesome group of people, who will spare themselves no effort to provide the counsellor with an opportunity of fulfilling his Christian duties. When such a situation arises, the counsellor must accept himself as a man, with definite limitations and frailties.

Only God has all the resources of the universe at his disposal. When the counsellor is found wanting he must not be too disconcerted by the pained reproach, 'I did not expect that of you!' Neither should he be unduly disconcerted by the client's close familiarity with the parable of the Good Samaritan. (Clients such as these conveniently misunderstand the parable of the Good Samaritan. They think of themselves in the role of the man who fell among thieves, and expect others to play the part of the Good Samaritan. They fail to appreciate that virtue is ascribed to the behaviour of the Samaritan, not to the victim.)

Patients from a different culture

Success in psychotherapy depends partly on the ease with which therapist and patient can communicate with each other. Attitudes, philosophies and behavioural patterns vary from one culture to another, and even though both may speak the same language, it may be difficult for a therapist from a different background to get on to the same 'wavelength' as his patient. If they do not share a common language, the difficulties are even more formidable. The therapist who is from a different culture will wish to do all that he can for his patient. But he should not under-estimate the difficulties. If it is possible the patient should be referred to a therapist from the same culture. When this is not possible, the difficulty of communication will be regarded as a significant anti-therapeutic factor. Otherwise the usual criteria of selection should be applied.

Parents and Relatives

When children are in need of treatment, parents will usually wish to be involved, although they may be frightened of the implications and anticipated criticisms. Parents frequently believe that psychological illness originates in 'faulty upbringing', and may be anxious that this should be so in their case. They will feel, usually with justification, that they have done their best. They will hope to be told 'exactly what the trouble is', and will expect the therapist to tell them, in a few brief words, how it can be put right.

The therapist may think it wise, in the first instance, to help parents whose child is suffering from a nervous illness to express their feelings about it. The discussion should certainly include their own sense of self-blame and their attempts to evade a feeling of responsibility. ('...my husband's uncle once had a nervous breakdown: could it be hereditary?')

Since parents rather expect to be blamed, they may be very much on the defensive. It is best for the therapist to avoid any semblance of criticism completely. When, to their relief, the parents discover that they are not to be scapegoated, much valuable information and assistance may be forthcoming.

Other relatives may offer information about the patient and may hope for information in return. The therapist should be careful not to reveal anything that is confidential. The reader is reminded that information obtained under a pledge of secrecy is of no value. If an informant says 'I am going to tell you something, but you must not say that I have told you', his offer must be firmly declined.

Sometimes, relatives come not to give information or help, but to make it clear that they have no help to offer. They often provide the well worn excuse, 'I am not well myself. I am under my doctor'. When this familiar evasion is voiced, there may be little to be gained from continuing with the discussion.

Relatives are often bothered by the question of how they should behave towards the patient, whilst he is being treated. Should they go out of their way to humour him? Should they make special allowances for him? If they feel angry with him, should they clench their teeth and count to ten? Insincere behaviour is usually detected by the patient very rapidly for the sham it is, and his reaction may be magnified in proportion. Relatives should, on the whole, behave in a which reflects how they truly feel: it is dishonest and unhelpful to try to behave otherwise. The patient must learn to cope with people as they really are, not as he would like them to be. It may be distressing for a while if the patient's wife tells him of her anger with him. But there is little point in not doing so if, at a later date, she has to confess that there are certain aspects of his behaviour which she dislikes, when for so long she has tolerated them without complaint.

You Cannot Win

There are certain patients with whom the therapist seems to find himself constantly at loggerheads. The most innocuous comment is turned into a battleground. Behaviour such as this often characterises the patient's whole life. He can relate with people only by fighting with them. It may become apparent to the therapist that he himself has fallen into the trap. Whatever he says seems to provoke the patient, and in his turn, whatever the patient says seems to provoke him. And, then, at the end of the day, he cries in despair 'You cannot win!' When this happens, it is necessary for the therapist to put to himself the question, 'Why do you want to win?' After all, psychotherapy is supposed to be constructive, not destructive: a collaboration, not a battle. The therapist who discovers that, imperceptibly, but inevitably he finds himself at loggerheads with his patient, must look first at his own part in the conflict. It is not sufficient merely to acknowledge that this is how the patient always handles *his* relationships. Why has it happened in this case? When the therapist has thought about his own contribution, it is appropriate for him to discuss with the patient 'How does it come about that you and I always seem to be at odds with one another?' When he has examined his own, the therapist is in a much better position to help the patient analyse his contribution.

The Eccentric

There are some people who do not wish to conform to the ordinary modes of life. This does not seem to be due to any failure of maturation or to any psychological abnormality, but because they prefer a way of life which others regard as eccentric. Such people are unlikely to come for therapy on their own account although their baffled friends and relatives may press them to do so. They may good-humouredly agree to participate, but therapy which is undertaken at the behest of someone else is/seldom of value, and the therapist may feel that something more than good-humoured compliance is needed if change is to be achieved. There seems little point in persevering with such cases.

The Flirtatious

Quite early in his career, the therapist will encounter patients or clients who seem to be more interested in developing a social or possibly a sexual relationship with the therapist than a professional one. It has already been stated that social relationships are not of help in psychotherapy: sexual relationships are even less so. If the therapist has embarked upon psychotherapy with a patient who proves to be flirtatious, he should take every opportunity to interpret the patient's attempts to change the nature of the relationship. He need not hesitate to speak openly about any sexual overtones.

Such cases are sometimes difficult, and can be very trying. The therapist should have no hesitation in consulting a more experienced colleague if he feels that he is getting out of his depth. If he does so, it is possible that he will be advised to discontinue the case, and when this advice is given, he should follow it. He may be greeted with the surprised reproof: 'You told me that I could say anything. Surely you didn't really think...?' But this reproof is usually voiced when the patient has failed to add a valuable scalp to his collection. The therapist need not feel too distressed.

Le Bovarysme

This is 'a condition occurring in dissatisfied young women, in whom a mixture of vanity, imagination, and ambition, has induced ideas above their station in life, especially in matters sentimental'.*

This condition is unlikely to be amenable to psychotherapy, but the syndrome is so beautifully described that the author could not resist the temptation to include it.

*Forfar and Benhaman, 'French-English Medical Glossary: I', The Lancet, Page 789, 6th October, 1973.

10. Termination

CARDINAL PRINCIPLE: *When all is finished, take care of the conscious, and leave the unconscious to take care of itself.*

Intensive psychotherapy continues for many months, and the patient often comes to assume that whenever a problem arises, he will always be able to discuss it with his therapist. He knows that the mere act of talking with an objective observer is helpful in teasing out some of the difficulties, even though a solution is not necessarily forthcoming. Thus, in the course of therapy, the patient becomes dependent on his therapist. This relationship is itself a neurotic one. The patient feels that he can always share his decisions and that he does not have to accept the sole and ultimate responsibility for them.

The neurotic dependence of the patient on his therapist is a necessary part of psychotherapy, and it gives him much courage to confront difficult areas of his life. When he faces a problem he feels that he has his therapist behind him. Sometimes he 'feels' this almost literally. It is as though the therapist were actually at his shoulder. He knows that he will be expected to report success or failure at their next meeting, and much of him wishes to report success. Occasionally the thought may come, 'How will I manage when I no longer have a therapist? What will happen when he says that I am not to come any more?' This is an uncomfortable thought, and the patient usually puts it out of his mind quickly. Sometimes, if things are going badly, and particularly if the patient believes that his therapist is feeling impatient or angry with him, he half expects to be told 'I don't want to see you any more'. This idea may be extremely frightening, and the patient will heave a sigh of relief when, despite the difficulties, an appointment is made for another session.

But a time must come when therapy has to finish. Sometimes this happens only when either the patient or the therapist dies, or when one moves so far away that communication between them becomes impossible. This may be very far away indeed. The patient who has a strong positive transference will think nothing of travelling the length of Great Britain in order to visit his therapist, as the author once discovered to his cost, whilst a colleague who went to work in Australia was greeted with delight by a patient whom he had thought was safely ensconced in Edinburgh.

Termination of psychotherapy should itself be regarded as part of psychotherapy, and it must be planned and executed with care. The patient will have to come to terms with the uncomfortable fact that a time is approaching when he must face his problems alone. The therapist must acknowledge that if his efforts have really been successful, his patient will sever all the bonds, and he will never know that things have gone well. He will never be able to pronounce the patient 'cured', for if he were to request him to come for review, it would mean that the therapeutic relationship was being continued. In psychotherapy, success is measured by the patient's ability to manage without a therapist.

If termination is to be an integral part of psychotherapy, it cannot be achieved during the course of one interview. The patient must be given sufficient time to work through his feelings about it. This process may require a number of sessions.

The author's practice is to allow about ten per cent of the time which has been allotted to therapy for the process of termination. If therapy has continued for twelve months, he allows five or six weeks for termination. His procedure is as follows:—

Towards the end of a session, preferably when an appropriate topic is being discussed, the therapist draws attention to the fact that eventually, therapy will have to come to an end. He emphasises that he wishes to share with his patient a decision about the timing of this, and asks him to consider it before their next meeting. Early in the next meeting he asks for his patient's ideas. Sometimes the patient will suggest that the meetings should cease forthwith, or in a very short time, but the therapist should not accept an abrupt termination. Alternatively, the patient may suggest a 'natural' finishing date. Perhaps the year is coming to an end, or a holiday is approaching, or such and such a date will be the anniversary of the commencement of therapy. If any of these suggestions fall within the 10 per cent rule, they may be accepted as appropriate.

The therapist will pay very great attention thereafter to themes which are concerned with parting, being left alone, death, starting a new life, being let down, and so on. There will be expressions of regret and resentment, feelings of being punished, attempts at 'making up'. There will also be expressions of gratitude for benefits which have been achieved. These things may be reported in respect of experiences from the past, but the therapist will have little difficulty in understanding that the latent content is directly associated with the intention to terminate. The patient is sorry that therapy is soon to stop, and grateful for the help that he has received, but he will be resentful at being left to manage without assistance, and may sometimes complain bitterly that he has derived no benefit from his attendance.

Occasionally these protestations may be difficult for the therapist to refute, and this may be particularly so when he feels that he has not helped his patient very much. In his turn he may be hurt and offended by what the patient says, but he must remember always that his instructions were that the patient should put into words all that he thought and felt. This, of course, is exactly what the patient is doing.

Therefore, although he may feel offended, the therapist must not protest or explain, or endeavour to compromise. The decision has been made, and it must be accepted. Incidentally, if it is really true that the patient has not benefited from many months of psychotherapy, then it is unlikely that he would be helped by many months more. His benefit is partly evidenced by the fact that he is actually able to *say*, 'I have not benefitted!'

Sometimes the patient will ask if he may return if special problems arise or if things go badly. Again the therapist must consider with care what such a request means. It may be a device for keeping the relationship alive. It implies that the patient will encounter situations for which he is not prepared. This is probably true, but it is to be questioned whether the patient can be made more prepared for the unexpected when he has already completed many months of therapy. The reply need not be an uncompromising negative, but the therapist should indicate his hope that the patient has learned sufficient about himself to allow him to cope with new problems from his own resources.

The patient will wonder what expectations the therapist will have of him. The therapist is equally anxious to know this, but it involves prediction, and the therapist will continue to emphasise that he is not a fortune teller. Only time can tell how the patient will manage, and it has already been indicated that the therapist himself may never know the answer.

The ultimate object of psychotherapy is to help the patient to 'grow' psychologically: to learn to face his problems as a healthy *adult*: to recognise that although he is not defenceless, he is responsible: that he does not need to turn personal problems into disease, and by so doing abrogate his own responsibility for them. If therapy has merely provided an alternative form of neurotic dependence, it has failed in its objective. The original contract was not that independence *would* be attained, but that the patient would be given help to attain it. The therapist's promise was that he would 'attend' to his patient; there was no promise that his problems would be solved.

Some therapists conclude the terminal phase of therapy with a period of weaning. The patient who has attended twice a week has the frequency of his sessions reduced to once a week, then to once a fortnight, then to once a month, then to once every three months. When this technique is employed, termination of treatment may continue for a very long period. The patient who is eventually seen only once in every three months, may continue to attend for several years. In these circumstances the sessions become little more than historical review of what has occurred since the previous meeting. Intensive therapy has drifted imperceptibly into supportive therapy, and the patient may never experience the apprehension or the exhilaration of facing a problem alone. Of course the therapist is able to keep a paternal eye upon his patient by maintaining the supportive relationship, but by doing so he is depriving the patient of one of the foremost aims of therapy: that of enabling him to manage without assistance.

When the patient comes to review the course of his treatment he will find that the intensity of many of the feelings that he once had: feelings of intense frustration, of affection, sometimes of dissatisfaction, sometimes of terrible fear: has disappeared. Often he finds himself quite unable to remember what actually occurred. He will realise that much that happened was obvious and that there was little that was really new: he will understand that he himself had to do most of the work. He will often feel a warm, but now rather remote affection for his therapist. He will find himself wanting to get in touch with him, perhaps to write to him. He seldom does.

In the last minutes of the last session, it is not uncommon for a patient to ask the therapist what he 'really thinks' of him. Perhaps he will ask a final favour, such as an opinion or a piece of advice. Such behaviour indicates a hope, maintained to the very end, that the therapist has some secret which he is withholding: something of value which he is keeping to himself. The request should be interpreted accordingly.

The final moments of therapy are rather nostalgic ones. But the therapist must emphasise that the last session is essentially the same as those that have gone before. He should in no way change his approach. When the patient leaves he may be given a conventional wish of good fortune. At this point the patient will occasionally press a gift into the hand of his therapist. Probably he should not accept; but to tell the truth he often does.

Despite what has been said, it is likely that the patient will get in touch with his therapist if a crisis should arise. If this happens only very occasionally, and in situations of obvious difficulty, the therapist will probably see the patient for a once-only session. On the other hand, if crises become commonplace they should be interpreted as a way of keeping open the dependent relationship. The difficulties and fears of breaking the chains of dependency may again be discussed with the patient. The therapist will then have to make a choice. Either he may refuse to see the patient any more, or he may accept that he is chronically dependent on him, and permit him to attend for periodic support. The therapist should not resume intensive psychotherapy. For the patient (although it is more difficult for the therapist) periodic support may be the better alternative. Occasionally, when the therapist accepts that he needs support, the patient acquires some belated independence. In such cases he is almost certainly going to demand support from someone, and perhaps that 'someone' should be the therapist, who knows him best.

Writing the last few words of a book like this is rather like terminating psychotherapy. The author has a warm, rather nostalgic feeling for the reader he will never meet. He is acutely aware of having written little that was not already obvious. He wonders why some readers have persevered to the end, whilst others could not get past the first page. He wonders how much more he should have included, and what he might have omitted. He wonders whether any of it has been useful and how much has been valueless. He hopes that some of his readers will write to tell him.

Index

Filmset in Hong Kong by T.P. Graphic Arts Services